FAITH, FAMILY, AND FORTUNE

FAITH, FAMILY, AND FORTUNE

Reformed Upbringing and Calvinist Values
of Highly Successful Dutch-American
Entrepreneurs

Peter Ester

Van Raalte
PRESS
Holland, Michigan

Van Raalte Press is a division of Hope College Publishing

Offices: Van Raalte Press
             Theil Research Center
             9 East 10th Street
             Holland, MI 49423

Mailing: Hope College
             PO Box 9000
             Holland, MI 49422-9000

vanraalte@hope.edu
www.hope.edu/vri

Printed in the United States of America

ISBN   978-1-7915420-5-4

Editor-in-chief and publisher: Jacob E. Nyenhuis, PhD
Copy editor: JoHannah Smith
Layout and cover design: Russell L. Gasero
Cover photos: Van Andel Soccer Stadium, courtesy Rob Kurtycz; all
      others, courtesy Hope College

Printed by: InnerWorkings, Grand Rapids, MI

In memory of my beloved parents
Jannes Ester and Hendrikje Mulder

Sociologist Peter Ester is a Lector at Rotterdam University and a Senator of the Kingdom of the Netherlands. He is a former Crown Member of the Social and Economic Council of the Netherlands; he previously was a professor and director of institutes for social research at both Utrecht University and the University of Tilburg, as well as Adjunct Research Professor at the A. C. Van Raalte Institute, Hope College.

The buildings on the cover are representative of the philanthropy of Dutch-American entrepreneurs; they do not necessarily represent any subjects of this study.

Contents

PART III

Results

Acknowledgments

I am greatly indebted to the twenty-one extraordinarily successful Dutch-American entrepreneurs who participated in this study. It is a truly remarkable sample of outstanding CEOs whose reputation and impact transcend the Michigan and even American economic borders. Without exception, they were very generous in giving me their valuable time for an often lengthy interview, in spite of busy and demanding agendas. It was a pleasure interviewing them on their upbringing, their youth memories, their values, their faith, and the way these essentials influenced their later success as an entrepreneur. All of them are business entrepreneurs who made a difference in life with respect to their company, their community, and their church: enterprising personalities in every sense.

I greatly appreciate the help of Van Raalte Institute Professors Donald J. Bruggink, Elton J. Bruins, Earl Wm. Kennedy, Jacob E. Nyenhuis, and Robert P. Swierenga, of Steve VanderVeen (Hope College), and Richard H. Harms (Calvin College), in compiling a short list of qualifying Dutch-American entrepreneurs and for supplying me with useful background information.

JoHannah Smith, office manager and editorial assistant of the Van Raalte Institute, did an extremely good job in arranging and scheduling the interviews. The interviews had to be conducted in the month of July 2010, and she succeeded in making all interview appointments in that narrow time slot. Her charming persistence undoubtedly resulted in an exceptionally high response rate. JoHannah also took care of the technical editing of this text in a most professional and helpful way. It was—as always—a joy working with her.

Many thanks to Brigid Maniates, JoHannah Smith, and Lori Trethewey for their outstanding job in transcribing the interviews—a job that takes a delicate combination of speed, dedication, and accuracy.

Finally, I am truly grateful to Jacob E. Nyenhuis, director of the Van Raalte Institute, for his inspiring support of this study, for his prudent help in approaching my highly profiled group of respondents, for "opening doors," and for creating excellent working conditions at the institute. The Van Raalte Institute has a uniquely friendly and scholarly atmosphere. In fact, the Van Raalte Institute is an institute of friendly scholars and scholarly friends.

Peter Ester
December 2011

Preface

I am pleased to present this latest publication of the Van Raalte Press, written by a former Netherland-America Foundation Visiting Research Fellow (2007) and former Adjunct Research Professor (2007-2011) at the Van Raalte Institute of Hope College. This is Peter Ester's second sociological study of Dutch-Americans in West Michigan, and it builds on his first, *Growing Up Dutch-American: Cultural Identity and the Formative Years of Older Dutch-Americans* (Van Raalte Press, 2008).

The methodology is the same for both of these ethnographic studies, for they are based on oral interviews conducted by a respected Dutch sociologist who has published over two hundred books and peer-reviewed journal articles on cross-national and intergenerational cultural and religious changes. One of his research interests—how ethnic-religious communities create and maintain sustainable social capital and the role of generations in transferring social capital—is an integral part of this study of highly successful Dutch-American entrepreneurs, as he explores the influence of a Reformed upbringing and fundamental Calvinist values upon these entrepreneurial leaders based in West Michigan.

It is fitting to use this opportunity to express my personal gratitude and the gratitude of the Van Raalte Institute to the subjects of this valuable study, the innovative leaders who so graciously responded to my letter asking them to welcome Dr. Ester into their offices or homes and to answer his wide-ranging questions that seek to understand and explain the factors that contributed to the tremendous success that they have enjoyed as entrepreneurs. Their willingness to provide honest, candid answers to these questions has made this study a highly valuable contribution to the literature on entrepreneurs and entrepreneurship.

This monograph further expands the range of studies conducted by members and visiting research fellows of the Van Raalte Institute, whose mission is to honor the memory and the vision of the Reverend Albertus C. Van Raalte, DD, by studying his life and work and by studying the contributions of the Dutch and their descendants in the United States of America. I invite you to visit our website (http://www. hope.edu/vri/) to learn more about the Institute and our extensive publications.

Jacob E. Nyenhuis
Director, Van Raalte Institute
Editor-in-Chief and Publisher,
Van Raalte Press

INTRODUCTION

For me, the greatest pleasure comes not from the endless acquisition of material things but from creating wealth and giving it away.

Jay Van Andel
An Enterprising Life (1998)

Remarkably Successful Dutch-American Entrepreneurs

West Michigan has a striking presence of successful Dutch-American enterprises or perhaps more accurate, enterprises founded by Dutch-Americans. Several of these companies turned into mega businesses. Jay Van Andel and his lifelong friend and business partner Richard DeVos founded Amway Corporation. The direct selling company—"a shining example of capitalism with a conscience" according to the late President Gerard R. Ford[1]—now operates in more than eighty countries and territories around the world, and enables more than three million people to own independent businesses. In 2007 annual sales were over $7 billion. The Meijer family started and still owns the Meijer Superstore chain which now includes over 190 stores in five states, sixty thousand employees, and annual sales over $12 billion. Prince Manufacturing, founded by Edgar Prince, produced automotive accessories, had a workforce of 4,500 employees, eight

[1]   President Gerald R. Ford foreward to *Rediscovering American Values. The Foundations of Our Freedom for the 21ˢᵗ Century* by Dick DeVos (New York: Plume, 1998).

1

production plants, and annual sales close to $1 billion. In 1996 it was sold to Johnson Controls. Herman Miller, Inc. started in 1905 under the leadership of D. J. De Pree as the Star Furniture Company in Zeeland, Michigan. It now is a major manufacturer of office furniture systems. The Miller Corporation has over six thousand employees and annual sales of about $2 billion.

These are four of the most appealing top-echelon examples of Dutch-American enterprises. The list becomes much longer if one includes smaller but still highly successful and profiled Michigan-based Dutch-American businesses such as Wolverine Gas & Oil Corporation (now merged with Dominion Resources, Inc.), SAF-Holland, Bouma Corporation, Kent Design and Manufacturing, Micro Machine Company, Hekman Furniture, ODL (Ottawa Door Light), Kool Chevrolet, Request Foods, A. C. Geenen Construction, and Eerdmans Publishing Company, to give just a few random examples.

Dutch-American entrepreneurs, so it seems, have done well.[2] They have left their mark on the West Michigan economy. Apparently, many of these industrialists and manufacturers have the right entrepreneurial skills to be highly competitive in a challenging and dynamic market. It is not only their business competency, however, that counts. Most of these Dutch-American entrepreneurs are committed Protestants, active members of Reformed churches, and firm believers in Calvinist doctrines. They see themselves as a part of the Reformed tradition that emphasizes the importance of a strong work ethic, the duty to use one's God given talents, the need for a modest lifestyle, the obligation to share one's wealth with others, and the commitment to community service and worthy causes. Their churches (the Reformed Church in America and the Christian Reformed Church) are strongly rooted in Dutch-American immigration history. Somehow, Calvinism and entrepreneurship go well together and, in combination, prosper in the American cultural context. To clarify this relationship is one of the main goals of this study.

Religion is an essential part of American society, and so is entrepreneurship. Entrepreneurship, in fact, is at the core of American culture: it champions personal success and economic dynamics. The entrepreneurial economy fits the American way of life well by

---

[2]   See also C. Carl Pegels, *Dutch-American Entrepreneurs. Their Contribution to American Society, Culture, and the Economy.* (School of Management, University at Buffalo, State University of New York, un-dated and unpublished manuscript). Downloadable via the New Netherlands Institute, Albany, NY and the New Netherlands Project (www. nnp.org/nni/Publications/dabook.html).

encouraging initiative, innovation, experimentation, and competition.[3] Entrepreneurship reflects the importance of autonomy, independence, and control. Starting a new business, starting one's *own* business, signals the American cultural primacy of being one's own boss, of self-determination, and of achievement. Seizing opportunity and being willing to take risks are part of the American entrepreneurial psychology. Failure is not perceived as a personal debacle—as it is in Europe—but as a challenge. In a highly individualized society such as the United States, entrepreneurship is the route *par excellence* to self-reliance, freedom, and success. In cases of extreme success—Bill Gates, Steve Jobs, Michael Dell, Ted Turner, Ben (Cohen) & Jerry (Greenfield), Larry Page, and Sergey Brin—entrepreneurial leaders become role models, heroes, and some even reach stardom. Free enterprise is the pillar of the entrepreneurial economic model. As Rich DeVos, one of the most successful Dutch-American entrepreneurs, states: "I am thankful every day for the rewards the free-enterprise system has provided to me and my family. I have worked hard, and I have enjoyed the rewards of my labor. Americans believe deeply in the benefits of hard work. It's part of our national psyche. And we believe in general, that a person is rewarded in proportion to their effort."[4]

Successful American entrepreneurs share a long history of being generous with their money; donating to charity, fund raising for good causes, endowing scholarships, and contributing to the community are all part of their cultural role in American society. Giving is certainly important to Dutch-American entrepreneurs. It is amazing how much they have donated to their communities, their churches, their schools and colleges, their students, and other important causes. Social responsibility is seen as a major part of the mission of many Dutch-American corporations. Historically, of course, the role of government and government programs differs markedly between the United States and Europe—which partly explains the tradition of corporate donations and services in America—but to a European observer, this intricate web of charity is phenomenal. Almost two centuries ago, French political thinker and historian Alexis de Tocqueville was already much impressed by the philanthropic spirit of Americans.[5] The donations amount to

---

[3] Cf. Council on Competitiveness, *Where America Stands: Entrepreneurship* (Washington, DC, 2007).

[4] Rich DeVos, *Compassionate Capitalism. People Helping People Help Themselves* (New York: Penguin Books, 1993), 95.

[5] Alexis de Tocqueville, *Democracy in America* (New York/Toronto: Alfred A. Knopf, 1993 [originally, 1835-40]).

billions of dollars, particularly in areas such as health, education, youth, the environment, social services, the arts, and religious causes.[6] But, as Fred Meijer stated: "I don't really think of it as generosity; I think it is just a way of looking at life. Each generation builds for the next one."[7]

Philanthropy has become big business in and of itself, even among Dutch-American entrepreneurs. A few telling examples: Jay Van Andel donated the Van Andel Museum, the Van Andel Arena, and the Van Andel Institute (devoted to medical research and education) to his hometown, Grand Rapids, Michigan. His business partner, Rich DeVos, contributed significantly to Christian schools in the Grand Rapids area; he was a major donor to the DeVos Center for Arts and Worship in Grand Rapids, the Grand Rapids Symphony, the Helen DeVos Children's Hospital, and Grand Valley State University's Cook DeVos Center for Health Sciences. He also bought and renovated (with Amway's co-founder Jay Van Andel) the Amway Grand Plaza hotel (the former Pantlind Hotel), a major renaissance of downtown Grand Rapids, and he built the adjacent Grand Center and DeVos Performance Hall. Fred Meijer was a major West Michigan benefactor, too.[8] He donated major funding to the Greenville Hospital, the Fred and Lena Meijer Heart Center in Grand Rapids, the Lena Rader Meijer Emergency Department of Kelsey Hospital in Lakeview, the Meijer Majestic Theater in Grand Rapids, the Meijer Public Broadcast Center and the Frederik Meijer Honors College at Grand Valley State University, the Hendrik and Gezina Meijer Surgery and Patient Care Center, the Fred Meijer Chair in Dutch Language and Culture at Calvin College, and the largest philanthropic project of his life: the Frederik Meijer Gardens and Sculpture Park. Edgar Prince, likewise, was the vision and driving force behind the successful revitalization of downtown

---

[6]   According to the Merrill-Capgemini 2010 World Wealth Report, North America's wealthiest donate about $200 billion annually. That figure comes from charitable contributions from people making $1 million or more.

[7]   Bill Smith and Larry ten Harmsel, *Fred Meijer: Stories of his Life* (Grand Rapids, MI: Eerdmans, 2009), 283.

[8]   This is how Meijer described his company's community involvement: "From developing community outreach programs to helping to preserve the environment, we are strongly committed to helping your community become a better place to live, work and play. We have long been a leader in helping build your communities, and our constant involvement has helped us feel part of your community. We care about you, strive to understand your family's needs, and cooperate with you and your community in order to provide the best service possible. We've done that by supporting communities we serve with local fundraisers, community events, donations, and resource development." (http://www.meijer.com). Fred Meijer died in December 2011 at the age of 91.—Ed.

Holland, Michigan, his hometown. He bought and renovated empty buildings, and recruited businesses, including numerous restaurants, to come to the area.[9]

The Foundation Center (New York City), whose mission it is to strengthen the nonprofit sector by advancing knowledge about United States philanthropy, calculated that in the fiscal year 2003, the Richard and Helen DeVos Foundation ranked sixth in the state of Michigan with total giving of $33 million; the Jay and Betty Van Andel Foundation took twelfth place with total donations of $15 million;[10] the Meijer Foundation ranked eighteenth with total giving of $9 million; and the Edgar and Elsa Prince Foundation took twenty-third place with total donations of $8 million.[11] Dutch-American entrepreneurs do well and donate well. As Jay Van Andel states: "The task of every person on earth is to use everything he is given, every ability he has, to the ultimate glory of God. . . . Just as in Jesus' parable, we are all custodians of all the material wealth we are given. Each individual is required to use his wealth to do good. . . . The dispersal of personal wealth is not a choice. Wealth must be given away."[12]

Quite a number of successful Dutch-American enterprises are family firms.[13] The Amway Corporation and Meijer are prime examples. Rich DeVos wrote in the early 1990s: "Today, all eight of the Van Andel and DeVos offspring are hard at work making this company better. . . . We meet monthly for brainstorming and long-range planning. Our children have become our peers in helping us guide this company, and each of them holds a special role in shaping Amway's future."[14] And as Hank Meijer, third generation co-chairman of Meijer, states: "Meijer remains a family company, as close to its origins as the scale of

---

9 *Money Magazine*, for several years in a row, has included Holland, MI among its list of the 25 best places to retire (www.money.cnn.com).

10 In regard to donating to social and religious causes, both the DeVos and Van Andel foundations are known for sponsoring conservative Christian pro-life initiatives. They clearly favor traditional ideas of morality and share Republican political beliefs.

11 The 2008 total assets were, respectively, the Richard and Helen DeVos Foundation: $77 million; the Meijer Foundation: $88 million; and the Edgar and Elsa Prince Foundation: $31 million. Source: The Foundation Center (New York City), www.foundationcenter.org. The Jay and Betty Van Andel Foundation was dissolved after Jay Van Andel's death in 2004.

12 Jay Van Andel, *An Enterprising Life: An Autobiography* (New York: HarperBusiness, 1998), 121-22.

13 Many large, even global, corporations are family-owned, e.g., Ford, Levi Strauss, Walmart, IKEA, Lego, Samsung, Tatas.

14 DeVos, *Compassionate Capitalism*, 234.

a large corporation allows."[15] Founding, developing, and maintaining a family firm requires robust entrepreneurship, that is, the regulation of ownership, management, and family relations. Many features are crucial to family firms, such as the issue of intergenerational succession, but a key quality is that those businesses are based on a primary network of social trust. Family ties create social capital that forms an ideal nucleus between the firm and the market. But the overlapping of family and business also creates a lot of potential conflicts. Balancing family dynamics and business interests is a continuous entrepreneurial test.[16] Culture, values, identity, and history are major and often essential facets of family firms. And this is quite true of Dutch-American family businesses given its origins in peculiar ethnic-religious communities.

Entrepreneurship seems to accommodate immigrant cultures favorably. Immigrant entrepreneurs have played a vital role in America's economic history, and they still do.[17] In 2005, 350 out of every one hundred thousand immigrants started a business per month, compared to 280 out of one hundred thousand native-born Americans. "Over the past 15 years, immigrants have started 25 percent of all US public venture-backed companies (including Intel, Sun Microsystems, eBay, Yahoo! and Google) as well as 46 percent of private venture-backed firms."[18] The current market capitalization of publicly traded immigrant-founded venture-backed companies in the United States exceeds $500

[15]   Hank Meijer, *Thrifty Years: The Life of Hendrik Meijer* (Grand Rapids, MI: Eerdmans, 1984 [reprinted 2008]), xi. In the afterword to the book, Hank Meijer adds: "In the half century since Hendrik's death, Meijer has grown dramatically. Annual sales have risen from $40 million in 1964 to more than $12 billion. Yet the company remains privately held, and its stockholders, all of whom are involved in the business, have chosen to reinvest profits in its future—its ability to grow and compete—rather than receive substantial dividends," 246.

[16]   See Kelin E. Gersick, John A. Davis, Marion McCollom Hampton, and Ivan Lansberg, *Generation to Generation: Life Cycles of the Family Business* (Cambridge, MA: Harvard Business School Press, 1997); Fred Neubauer and Alden G. Lank, *The Family Business: Its Governance for Sustainability* (Basingstoke: MacMillan Press, 1998); Andrea Colli and Mary Rose, "Family Business," in: Geoffrey Jones and Jonathan Zeitlin, *The Oxford Handbook of Business History* (Oxford: Oxford University Press, 2008).

[17]   See John S. Butler & George Kozmetsky, eds., *Immigrant and Minority Entrepreneurship: The Continuous Rebirth of American Communities* (Westpoint, CT: Prager Publishers, 2005); Richard T. Herman and Robert L. Smith, *Immigrant, Inc.: Why Immigrant Entrepreneurs are Driving the New Economy (and How They Will Save the American Worker)* (Hoboken, New Jersey: John Wiley and Sons, Inc., 2009); Center for an Urban Future, *A World of Opportunity* (New York City, NY, 2007).

[18]   National Venture Capital Association. *American Made. The Impact of Immigrant Entrepreneurs and Professionals on U. S. Competitiveness* (Arlington, VA, 2009).

billion, adding substantial value to the American economy.[19] In a rapidly globalizing economy, successful entrepreneurship is a major competitive and comparative advantage. America thrives on entrepreneurship. As an immigrant society, its economic ethos and psychological mores are well on par with the entrepreneurial spirit. Entrepreneurship, in short, is in America's cultural genes.

The business ventures of Dutch-American entrepreneurs seem to be imbued by this spirit as well. Their religious beliefs, as I will argue, are a major resource on which this spirit flourished. Dutch-American tycoon Rich DeVos asserts: "for Jay [Amway's co-founder Jay Van Andel] and me, it was never enough to believe in ourselves. We also believed in a loving creator whose dreams for us were far greater than any dreams we could have on our own. Now look at what we—God and all of us—have done together . . . the tools of capitalism and the goods and services that have been produced are a direct result of God's invitation to each of us to subdue and to use the products of our hands and hearts to honor our creator."[20] The Calvinist credo and capitalism seem to go well together. Understanding this relationship in more detail is the main objective of this study.

The Plan of the Book

Part I reflects on the successful blending of Calvinism and capitalism as a main feature of Dutch-American entrepreneurship. Chapter one describes the peculiar background of Dutch Protestant group immigration to America, particularly in the nineteenth century. The chapter analyzes Max Weber's views on how Protestantism, entrepreneurship, and capitalism are historically and culturally interconnected. Weber's work is a classic, and he is the most influential social scientist on this intriguing subject. Chapter two examines the views of two icons in the study of entrepreneurship: Jospeh Schumpeter and Peter Drucker, and it explores the various dimensions of the entrepreneurial mindset. The main research questions are outlined in chapter four: the linkage between Reformed faith, Dutch heritage, and entrepreneurial success.

Part II provides information on the methodology of this study. Chapter four reports the details of the interviews, the sample of highly successful Dutch-American CEOs, and the method of personal interviews. Part III gives the main results of this research. Chapter five

---

[19]   Center for an Urban Future, *A World of Opportunity*, 5.
[20]   DeVos, *Compassionate Capitalism*, 250.

presents how CEOs look back at their youth: their upbringing, their values, and the role of the church. It raises the vital question of how essentials of their formative period are related to their later success as an entrepreneur. In chapter six, the beliefs of the CEOs are investigated in terms of how their basic norms and values influence their risk-taking, their corporate strategy, and the customer orientation and personnel policy of their company. Does faith make a difference here? Chapter seven considers the views of the CEOs and the way in which their fundamental religious convictions impact their personal lifestyle, their involvement in charity and philanthropy, and their political opinions. What is the role of the Calvinist credo in these domains? The main conclusions of this study are summarized and put into perspective in chapter eight. Do a firm Reformed worldview and a solid Dutch background have a distinctive impact on entrepreneurial excellence? Do faith, family, and fortune go well together?

PART I

DUTCH-AMERICAN ENTREPRENEURSHIP:
BLENDING CALVINISM AND CAPITALISM

CHAPTER 1

Dutch Immigration, Reformed Faith, and Entrepreneurship

Dutch Immigration: Entrepreneurial Reformed Communities

The Dutch-American business ventures mentioned in the previous chapter are certainly impressive cases of first- and second-generation-immigrant entrepreneurship. Whether the figures are more or less comparable to other ethnic immigrant groups is unclear and difficult to assess. What is clear, however, is that most Dutch immigrants in the nineteenth century came to settle as farmers and not as business entrepreneurs. "Throughout the nineteenth century, Dutch overseas emigration was overwhelmingly a folk migration of rural families seeking cheap land in the United States."[1] Calculations by historian and Dutch immigration specialist Professor Robert P. Swierenga show that, from 1835 throughout 1880, the vast majority of immigrants consisted of farmers, farm laborers, craftsmen, and other laborers, and most came from rural areas in the provinces of Zeeland, Groningen, Friesland, and Gelderland. About 80 percent of Dutch immigrants moved

[1] Robert P. Swierenga, *Faith and the Family: Dutch Immigration and Settlement in the United States, 1820-1920* (New York/London: Holmes & Meier, 2000), 35.

11

from rural areas. "Quite obviously, the promise of low-priced land in America held greater allure to the Dutch peasant folk than business and professional opportunities in the states appealed to the urban middle-class. Only 20 percent of all overseas emigrants were of urban origin, and few of these went to America."[2] Swierenga's calculations show furthermore that there was little occupational diversity and job specialization among Dutch immigrants, which in essence indicates a pre-industrial workforce. Typical occupations in the non-farming domain include carpenter, shoemaker, baker, sailor, and weaver. Non-blue-collar immigrant occupations were a minority; Dutch immigrants with a white collar background (merchants, businessmen, shopkeepers, and professionals) were greatly under-represented and never accounted for more than ten percent in the 1835-80 emigration period. Although emigration itself is an act that requires a lot of entrepreneurship and risk-taking, commercial entrepreneurs themselves were a minority among Dutch immigrants. In terms of social class, about two-thirds of Dutch immigrants could be typified as neither "needy" nor "well-to-do" (22 and 11 percent, respectively).[3] The conclusion is clear: agricultural and blue-collar workers made up the majority of Dutch immigrants in the nineteenth century. This pattern is related to a variety of push factors in Dutch society in the nineteenth century that caused Dutch farmers and craftsmen to seek relief overseas: harvest failures, potato crisis, food shortages, labor surplus, fast population growth, land redistribution and land lease policies, high national debt and high taxes, chronic unemployment, low wages, high prices, pauperism, the formation of a rural proletariat, economic stagnation, meager economic prospects, and widespread feelings of relative deprivation.[4] These were the main social and economic factors that rapidly fueled the transatlantic emigration fever, resulting in a total of fifty-five thousand Dutch emigrants to the United States in the years between 1835 and 1880.[5]

---

[2]   Ibid., 43.
[3]   Immigrants with a Seceder background were, relatively speaking, most affluent, followed by Catholic immigrants.
[4]   Swierenga, *Faith and the Family*, chapter 1. See also Jacob Van Hinte, *Netherlanders in America: A Study of Emigration and Settlement in the Nineteenth and Twentieth Centuries in the United States of America* (in Dutch, 2 vols. Groningen: Noordhof, 1928), Robert P. Swierenga, gen. ed. Adriaan de Wit, chief transl. (Grand Rapids: Baker Book House, 1985); Hans Krabbendam, *Freedom on the Horizon: Dutch Immigration to America 1840-1940* (Grand Rapids, MI: Eerdmans, 2009); Pieter R. D. Stokvis. *De Nederlandse Trek naar Amerika. 1846-1847* (Leiden, NL: Universitaire Pers Leiden, 1977).
[5]   Between 1880 and 1920, another 130,000 Dutch people would emigrate to the United States.

Dutch immigration to America was not only specific in terms of region, occupation, and class, but also, and perhaps even more so, in terms of religion. A look at the religious affiliation of Dutch immigrants in the 1835 to 1880 period shows a revealing pattern. A substantial majority of 65 percent belonged to the *Hervormde Kerk* (Reformed Church), 20 percent were Catholics, 13 percent were Seceders (*Afgescheidenen*) from the *Hervormde Kerk*, and 2 percent were Jews. This pattern does not reflect the actual distribution of religious affiliation in the Netherlands in that period. Both *Hervormden* and Seceders were *over*-represented among the immigrants and Catholics were *under*-represented.[6] The Seceders split off from the *Hervormde Kerk* in 1834, since they opposed the prevailing spirit of rationalism and liberalism, the departure from Reformed orthodoxy and spiritual authority, the weakening of Reformed sacraments and church practices, the neglect of church discipline, the worldliness of Reformed pastors, and the growing interference with the Dutch state in church affairs. In the eyes of the Seceders, the Dutch Reformed Church had turned into a "false church," and by their secession, they therefore were returning to orthodoxy and orthopraxy, and were re-establishing the "true church."

Though the Seceders made up only a small proportion of the Dutch emigration wave in the nineteenth century, the religious-group nature of their emigration and their settlement of rural "Dutch" colonies in Holland, Michigan and in Iowa (Pella) and Wisconsin (Sheboygan) gave them a very recognizable status. They founded their communities based on their Seceder identity, that is, on their religious beliefs and values. Their religion and their churches were the backbone of their colonies, the cement, so to speak of their social system. Their Calvinist heritage strongly dictated the settlements' culture and institutions. The Dutch Seceder immigrants came as an ethnic religious group—often as congregations—and settled as an ethnic religious group. Their leaders were *religious* leaders, pastors from their Seceder churches in the Netherlands: Albertus Van Raalte and his followers founded the Holland, Michigan settlement; Hendrik P. Scholte and his people established the Pella, Iowa colony. After their arrival in the 1840s, the Seceder immigrants started to build and organize their agricultural communities, their churches, and their schools, and they started their small businesses, newspapers, and organizations. Evidently, the building of their colonies required substantial entrepreneurship of the

6   Robert P. Swierenga, "Dutch Immigration Patterns in the Nineteenth and Twentieth Century," in *The Dutch in America. Immigration, Settlement, and Cultural Change* (New Brunswick: Rutgers University Press, 1985) 15-42.

Dutch settlers, both collectively and individually. They had to adjust to their new natural habitat (soil, climate, fauna) and cultural environment (people, language, customs), to build an infrastructure (houses, town, roads), to set up their farms and start businesses, to establish the colony administration (rules, procedures, decision making, officials), to establish a school system, to regulate contacts with the outside world, and perhaps most importantly, to restart and redefine their religious life and institutions.[7]

Their shared history and their group emigration and settlement reinforced the "clannish" nature of Dutch immigrant colonies. But it also added to its relatively strong social capital by which they were able to maintain their core cultural identity and religious character.[8] Strong community ties, a basic sense of a shared past, present, and destiny, strict religious self-perceptions and in-group/out-group attitudes, firm socialization practices, and physical proximity, nurtured and sustained their ethnic and religious distinctiveness. Having solid social capital was and is a major factor that explains the survival of Dutch immigrant settlements. But building their communities also generated social capital: it is both an antecedent *and* a consequence. Social capital and collective entrepreneurship are mutually reinforcing.[9]

Individual entrepreneurship also benefits from a collective entrepreneurial spirit, because its embeddedness in a community context of significant social capital creates high trust, and vice versa. In an immigration environment that is characterized by uncertainty, insecurity, and fundamental existential challenges, high trust is a solid condition for entrepreneurial activities. A high trust community is critical to economic prosperity.[10] Social capital and high trust represented cultural conditions that were reinforced by the group nature and specific religious background of Dutch immigration to America. Community leadership that is actively pro-entrepreneurship

---

[7]   See Van Hinte, *Netherlanders in America*, chapters 7 and 8.

[8]   See Peter Ester, "Still Bowling Together: Social Capital of Dutch Protestant Immigrant Groups in North America," in George Harinck and Hans Krabbendam, eds., *Morsels in the Melting Pot. The Persistence of Dutch Immigrant Communities in North America* (Amsterdam: VU University Press, 2006), 21-31.

[9]   Donna Marie De Carolis and Patrick Saparito, "Social Capital, Cognition, and Entrepreneurial Opportunities: A Theoretical Framework," in *Entrepreneurship Theory and Practice* 30 (2006): 41-56.

[10] Francis Fukuyama, *Trust: The Social Virtues and the Creation of Prosperity* (London: Penguin Books, 1996). See also, Sjoerd Beugelsdijk, "Social Capital and Growth in European Regions: An Empirical Test," in *European Journal of Political Economy*, 21 (2005): 301-14; "Trust and Economic Growth: A Robustness Analysis," in *Oxford Economic Papers* 56 (2002): 118-34.

is, no doubt, also decisive. This was obviously the case in the nineteenth century Dutch immigration settlements. Both Van Raalte and Scholte were entrepreneurial settlement leaders with a keen eye for business opportunities for their community and for themselves.[11] This is how Swierenga characterizes Van Raalte as a businessman: "He had the instincts of an entrepreneur and was a risk taker. It was a life-long pattern. Van Raalte had a dynamic view of money and always tried to put ready cash to work, expecting to earn market rate of interest on his investments. From his late twenties and continuing until his last years, Van Raalte was involved in various business ventures in manufacturing, milling, retailing, newspaper publishing, and especially real estate and mortgage lending."[12] Securing land for the settlement demanded his primary attention, but he was also involved in a series of economic enterprises that were of great importance for the development of the colony. Pioneer leader Scholte was perhaps even a more typical Protestant entrepreneur in the classic sense. He was already well-to-do before he immigrated to America.[13] Scholte—named the "Hollanders' prophet, priest, and king"[14]—built his family an aristocratic house in the Pella settlement and, besides being a minister, was engaged in a wide variety of business ventures: land estate, real estate, banking, local industry, the bar, insurance, publishing. He combined his energetic business activities with being involved in politics, the notary public, and higher education. Scholte was increasingly subject to criticism by his followers, particularly because of his multifarious commercial dealings and lifestyle.[15]

[11] Henk Aay and Peter Ester, "A Case of Perception Bias—Jacob Van Hinte's Views on Albertus C. Van Raalte and Hendrik P. Scholte as Dutch Immigrant Leaders," paper presented at the International Bilateral Conference, "Albertus C. Van Raalte, Leader and Liaison," celebrating the A. C. Van Raalte Bicentennial (1811-2011). Organized by Hope College, A. C. Van Raalte Institute and VU University Amsterdam, VU Historical Documentation Centre. At Hope College: 24-25 October 2011. At Landgoed Het Laer, Ommen, the Netherlands: 3-4 November 2011.

[12] Robert P. Swierenga, "Albertus C. Van Raalte as a Businessman," in *A Goodly Heritage: Essays in Honor of the Reverend Dr. Elton J. Bruins at Eighty*, ed. Jacob E. Nyenhuis (Grand Rapids, MI: Eerdmans, 2007), 281-317. Swierenga estimates Van Raalte's land investment portfolio worth $5 million in today's dollars.

[13] Scholte received a considerable inheritance when his father (a manufacturer) died.

[14] See Henry S. Lucas, *Netherlanders in America* (Ann Arbor, MI: University of Michigan Press, 1955), 190.

[15] See Lubbertus Oostendorp, *H. P. Scholte. Leader of the Secession of 1834 and Founder of Pella* (Franeker: Wever, 1964). See also Arnold Mulder, *Americans from Holland* (Philadelphia and New York, J. P. Lippincott Company, 1947), 185-88; Harvey W. Noordsy, "Lourens van Bergeijk's Pamphlet Defense of Hendrik P. Scholte," in: Robert P. Swierenga, Jacob E. Nyenhuis & Nella Kennedy, eds., *Dutch-American Arts and Letters in Historical Perspective* (Holland, MI: Van Raalte Press, 2008). See also Henk Aay and Peter Ester, "A Case of Perception Bias," 2011.

After starting under very difficult and challenging circumstances, the larger Dutch settlements generally prospered. This is certainly true for the Holland, Michigan colony.[16] At the end of the nineteenth century, the colony rapidly industrialized. Examples of factories include the Cappon and Bertsch Leather Company, the Holland Shoe Company, the Ottawa Furniture Company, Holland Furniture Company, Holland Lumber and Supply Company, C. L. King Basket Factory, Superior Pure Ice and Machine Company, Western Michigan Tool Works, Launch and Engine Company, the Bay View Furniture Company, the Bush and Lane Piano Company, Holland Furnace Company, De Pree Chemical Company, Beach Milling Company, the Standard Milling and Grocer Company, Holland Sugar Company, Holland Rusk Company, Holland Maid Company, and the H. J. Heinz Factory.[17] Private banks aided the growth of Holland's industrial base and connected prominent local families. Three of the most important local banks were the Holland City Bank, First State Bank, and the Peoples State Bank.

A seminal factor in the rapid development and industrialization of the Holland area settlement, according to Van Hinte in his *magnum opus* on Dutch immigration in America, was "the favorable reputation that was particularly ascribed to the Calvinistic Hollanders. They were deemed to be very suited for factory work, since they were highly trustworthy, they had a strong sense of duty, and they completely lacked any tendencies towards class struggles."[18] This assumed relationship between Calvinist beliefs, work ethic, and entrepreneurship has a marked history in the social sciences and was most pronouncedly elaborated by Max Weber, to whom I will turn now.

Max Weber on Protestantism, Entrepreneurship, and Capitalism

Max Weber (1864-1920), one of the founding fathers of modern sociology, explicitly thematized the relationship between Protestantism,

[16]   In the early days of the Holland Colony, the land west of River Avenue between 1st and 8th Streets was Holland's business center. Businesses on this narrow strip included Van Raalte and Henry Post's salt, soap, and soda factory, Vander Sluis's stream-driven flour and sawmill, Peter Pfanstiehl's tannery, and Jacob Van Putten's butter tub factory. See: Steve Vanderveen et al., *The Leaders Next Door: A History of the Holland-Zeeland Area,* (Institute for Project-based Learning, Hope College, Holland, MI: 2007), 18.

[17]   Examples listed by Van Hinte, *Netherlanders in America,* 775-79 and by Steve Vanderveen et al., *The Leaders Next Door.*

[18]   Van Hinte, *Netherlanders in America,* 775. See also Peter Ester, Nella Kennedy, and Earl Wm. Kennedy, *The American Diary of Jacob Van Hinte. Author of the Classic Immigrant Study "Nederlanders in Amerika,"* (Holland/Grand Rapids, MI: Van Raalte Press/Eerdmans, 2010), part 1.

entrepreneurship, and economic development. His mental legacy is highly instrumental in understanding the success of Dutch-American entrepreneurs. In his landmark *The Protestant Ethic and the Spirit of Capitalism*, first published in 1904, Weber argued that the relatively rapid economic development of the Occident was made possible by both the rational and puritan Calvinist manner of thinking and way of life. The post-Reformation Protestant ethic was the perfect breeding ground on which the spirit of capitalism and entrepreneurship could flourish. Weber explained the economic rise of Western societies such as England, Germany, the Netherlands, and the American colonies in the seventeenth and eighteenth centuries in terms of their dominant puritan Calvinist *Weltanschauung*, their prevalent Protestant worldview. Capitalism and Calvinism encourage similar personal values fostering entrepreneurship and economic development. The essential feature of capitalist entrepreneurship is its rational and disciplined organization of "free labor" and its regularization of capital investment. Entrepreneurship and economic development are not just means to satisfy material needs but are acts in their own right. The investment and re-investment of capital, economic acquisition and reproduction, and rationalization and efficiency all set modern capitalist economies apart from traditional economies.

The *summum bonum* of the capitalist spirit, according to Weber, is not the hedonistic enjoyment of material goods but the rational and disciplined earning of money. "Man is dominated by the making of money, by acquisition as the ultimate purpose of his life. Economic acquisition is no longer subordinated to man as the means for the acquisition of his material needs."[19] The Alpha and Omega of the spirit of capitalism is rooted in the peculiar set of religious values that distinguished puritan Calvinist groups from other religions (for example, Catholicism, Hinduism, Buddhism, Confucianism). Capitalism is about success and not merely about profit. It is exactly at this point that Weber stresses the intrinsic correspondence (*Wahlverwandtschaft*) between the capitalist spirit and the Calvinist ethic. Calvinism does not encourage greed and hedonism, but it does recognize that worldly success is a sign of virtue and of God's election. The Protestant doctrine of predestination—the *decretum horribile*—leaves man in a state of uncertainty with respect to his eternal salvation or damnation. God, in his absolute sovereign authority, has preordained some people to eternal rescue and others to

---

[19]   Max Weber, *The Protestant Ethic and the Spirit of Capitalism*, (Oxford: Routledge, 2007 [first published 1930 by Allen and Unwin]), 18.

everlasting death. Every attempt by man to know or doubt God's will is an invasion of his sovereignty (the dogma of the hidden God—*deus absconditus*). Worldly success, however, may reflect that one belongs to the chosen, and may point toward a calling by God himself.

Calvinism contributed to the rationalization of the world by the elimination of magic as a form of salvation. Certainty of forgiveness, atonement and release, and absolution are concepts which are at odds with Calvinist theology. The banning of magic led to an increased emphasis on rationality, calculation, and planning—qualities that are at the very heart of the capitalist entrepreneurial spirit. In this sense the rationalization process as advocated by the Protestant way of thinking led to a fundamental disenchantment of the world.

The correspondence between the Protestant ethic and the capitalist spirit is not only a matter of worldview but also of conduct. The various Calvinist groups in countries such as England, Germany, the Netherlands, and the American colonies strongly emphasized a "this-worldly asceticism" (*innerweltliche Askese*), that is, a frugal lifestyle. These puritan groups and sects (Reformed, Mennonites, Methodists, Baptists) preached personal values such as order, diligence, hard work, discipline, self-control, saving, austerity, and seriousness. These values were firmly rooted in Calvinist theology and were to be practiced in the world and for the sake of the world—unlike the inner directed monastic forms of asceticism. Alternatively, values such as laziness, relaxation, enjoyment of wealth with idleness, and temptations of the flesh as consequences, distract the Calvinist from the righteous life. Work is a holy duty. The calling by God is fundamental in how to lead a righteous life. Economic success is a practical indication of such a calling. "For if that God, whose hand the Puritan sees in all the occurrences of life, shows one of His elect a chance for profit, he must do so with a purpose. Hence the faithful Christian must follow the call by taking advantage of the opportunity."[20] Wealth as a result of following God's call is not a sin but a blessing and a possible sign of being among the chosen. "Wealth is thus bad ethically only in so far as it is a temptation to idleness and sinful enjoyment of life, and its acquisition is bad only when it is with the purpose of later living merrily and without care. But as a performance of duty in a calling, it is not only morally permissible, but actually enjoined."[21] The accumulation of personal wealth was morally legitimized, because it was combined with a frugal lifestyle.

[20]   Ibid., 108.
[21]   Ibid., 108.

This blending of ascetic and entrepreneurial values, according to Weber, has been crucial in the rise of capitalism in the West. "The religious valuation of restless, continuous, systematic work in a worldly calling, as the highest means to asceticism, and at the same time the surest and most evident proof of rebirth and genuine faith, must have been the most powerful conceivable lever for the expansion of that attitude toward life, which we have here called the spirit of capitalism. When the limitation of consumption is combined with this release of acquisitive activity, the inevitable practical result is obvious: accumulation of capital through ascetic compulsion to save."[22] Calvinism, in short, provided the moral spirit, energy, and drive for the modern capitalist entrepreneur.

Weber regarded Founding Father Benjamin Franklin as a typical exponent of the capitalistic spirit and the Protestant ethic. He analyzed the ethical principles underlying two of Franklin's famous writings: *Necessary Hints to Those that Would Be Rich* (1737) and *Advice to a Young Tradesman* (1748). Being a good businessman, according to Franklin, implied adhering to a number of vital principles such as industry (time is money) and frugality, punctuality and honesty (credit is money), not wasting money on needless things, careful calculations, and not letting money go unused (even small investments can generate profits). Weber emphasized that these principles are not just an indication of entrepreneurial cleverness or purely egocentric purposes, but they form an *ethic* in which hard work and seeking profits go together with rejecting a hedonistic lifestyle. This combination is the nucleus of how Calvinism paved the way for modern capitalism.

The *Protestant Ethic and the Spirit of Capitalism* is a classic masterpiece of sociological thought and one of the most influential studies in the social sciences. It met with praise initially, but it also started an intellectual debate that continues even now. This is, however, not the place to reconstruct the debate and the critical issues and controversies that were raised.[23] For our study on the values of Reformed Dutch-American entrepreneurs, the most important Weberian notion is the correspondence between Calvinist thought and capitalist entrepreneurship in terms of values, worldview, and lifestyle.

[22]   Ibid., 116.
[23]   See the introduction by Anthony Giddens to the *Protestant Ethic and the Spirit of Capitalism* in which he identifies five major points of criticism: Weber's characterization of Protestantism, his interpretation of Catholic doctrines, Weber's empirical evidence for the connections between Puritanism and capitalism, his classification of modern and pre-modern capitalist activity, and the nature of causality between Puritanism and capitalism (Routledge Classics, 2001), xx1-xxiii.

It will be of interest to see if our sample of highly successful Dutch-American entrepreneurs identifies with these values, the worldview, and the lifestyle, and recognizes the ties between Calvinism and capitalism, not so much in terms of actual behavior and achievements but more in terms of subjective assessments.

Weber himself was rather concerned about the future of capitalism as he observed a decoupling of the capitalist spirit and religious asceticism. This is particularly true for the United States, where "the pursuit of wealth, stripped of its religious and ethical meaning, tends to become associated with pure mundane passions."[24] This reflects a fundamental paradox: the development of capitalism was enabled by the Protestant ethic but in contemporary society "victorious capitalism . . . needs its support no longer."[25] Is this erosion of the Calvinist basis of the capitalist spirit as well observable among Dutch-American entrepreneurs who are tried and tested in the Reformed tradition? Or is their pursuit for entrepreneurial success still firmly rooted in the Protestant ethic? Before addressing these elementary questions, however, we need to reflect on the essence of entrepreneurship. First, in regard to its theoretical assumptions, and second, with respect to some of its empirical dimensions and correlates.

---

[24] Weber, *The Protestant Ethic and the Spirit of Capitalism*, 124. In 1904 Weber made a study trip, with his wife Marianne and German Protestant theologian Ernst Troelstch, to the United States visiting, among other places, New York, Chicago, Oklahoma, New Orleans, and St. Louis (which hosted the World's Fair). At the library of Columbia University, he consulted several sources for his study on the Protestant ethic. See Marianne Weber and Max Weber, *A Biography* (New Brunswick: Transaction Books, 1988).

[25] Weber, *The Protestant Ethic and the Spirit of Capitalism*, 124.

CHAPTER 2

The Entrepreneurial Mindset

Entrepreneurship and Economic Development: Joseph Schumpeter

The way entrepreneurship is related to economic development and innovation has been most clearly conceptualized by two icons of economic and management thought: Joseph A. Schumpeter and Peter F. Drucker. Schumpeter (1883-1950) left his mark by putting the human agent at center stage in economic development, and Drucker (1909-2005), the founding father of the study of management, impressed us by his analysis of how successful innovation and successful entrepreneurship are interwoven.

Schumpeter gave a prominent role to the entrepreneur in his theory of economic development.[1] He described the entrepreneur in an almost romantic, even heroic fashion:

"First of all there is the dream and the will to found a private kingdom, usually, though not necessarily, also a dynasty.... Then

---

[1] James A. Schumpeter, *The Theory of Economic Development*, (Cambridge, MA: Harvard University Press, 1934); James A. Schumpeter, *Capitalism, Socialism and Democracy* (New York: Harper, 1943).

there is the will to conquer: the impulse to fight, to prove oneself superior to others, to succeed for the sake, not of the fruits of success, but of success itself. From this aspect, economic action becomes akin to sport. . . . The financial result is a secondary consideration, or, at all events, mainly valued as an index of success and as a symptom of victory, the displaying of which very often is more important as a motive of large expenditure than the wish for the consumers' goods themselves. . . . Finally, there is the joy of creating, of getting things done, or simply of exercising one's energy and ingenuity. . . . Our type seeks out difficulties, change in order to change, delights in ventures."[2]

What is of interest in Schumpeter's definition, is that entrepreneurship is intrinsically motivated: the entrepreneur is guided by being successful and innovative, by being dynamically involved in change, and by breaking established routines. Extrinsic rewards, such as greater wealth, are less important. The entrepreneur seeks new paths, is a non-conformist, is of unusual will, enjoys creative challenges, and treasures autonomy and independence. He knows how to withstand opposition and is forward-looking. Schumpeter's entrepreneur is a visionary and proactive leader who takes pleasure in achieving inspiring goals. Innovative and revolutionary entrepreneurship generates creative capitalism, but it also eliminates obsolete industries. New firms based on dynamic and entrepreneurial leadership displace less innovative incumbents. Schumpeter termed this the "creative destruction" of the free market.[3] In this sense innovative business leadership is a vital force in industrial restructuring.

Entrepreneurship and Innovation: Peter Drucker

Peter Drucker, the much celebrated management guru, influenced generations of managers with his thoughts on innovation and entrepreneurship. Drucker saw innovation as a major tool of entrepreneurs to exploit change: "The entrepreneur always searches for change, responds to it, and exploits it as an opportunity."[4] Entrepreneurs create new products, new markets, and new customers.

---

[2]   Schumpeter, *Economic Development*, 93-94.
[3]   The term itself was first used by German economist and sociologist Werner Sombart (1863-1941) in his book *Krieg und Kapitalismus* (War and Capitalism) (Leipzig: Duncker & Humblot, 1913, 207).
[4]   Peter F. Drucker, *Innovation and Entrepreneurship. Practice and Principles* (Amsterdam/Boston: Elsevier/Butterworth-Heinemann, 2009 [first edition 1985]), 25.

Entrepreneurship is not confined to small businesses or large businesses; it is not limited to the economic sphere, for it applies to both the profit and non-profit sector. Drucker emphasized that entrepreneurship was not a personality trait: "in thirty years I have seen people of the most diverse personalities and temperaments perform well in entrepreneurial challenges."[5] The idea of an entrepreneurial personality is a myth. What successful entrepreneurs do is to create new and different values; they are not satisfied with merely improving what already is. They go for the new and different; they seize the right opportunity at the right time. Systematic innovation is essential in this process which consists "in the purposeful and organized search for changes, and in the systematic analysis of the opportunities such changes might offer for economic or social innovation."[6] Entrepreneurs exploit change and monitor areas and sources for innovative opportunity, including unexpected successes or failures, incongruities between what is and what ought to be, innovation based on process need, changes in industry or market structure, demographic changes, changes in perceptions, and the availability of new knowledge.

Common sense dictates that innovations based on a bright idea are the most successful source of innovations. Drucker argued, however, that bright ideas were among the riskiest and least successful innovations. "The casualty rate is enormous."[7] He estimated that one out of every one hundred patents earned enough to pay back development costs, and that one out of five hundred innovations made any money above its out-of-pocket costs. Most bright ideas turn out to be vague, elusive, and unpredictable. Nevertheless, according to Drucker, we must cherish this category of innovations, since bright ideas reflect the qualities society needs: "initiative, ambition, and ingenuity."[8] Drucker outlined a number of principles that entrepreneurs need to apply for innovations to be successful: (1) opportunities need to be systematically analyzed; (2) innovation is both conceptual and perceptual; (3) an innovation needs to be simple and focused; (4) effective innovations start small; and (5) successful innovations aim at leadership. These principles will only be effective under certain conditions: innovation is (hard) work; to succeed, innovators must build on their strengths; and an innovation has an effect on economy and society and therefore must be market-driven.

[5]   Ibid., 23.
[6]   Ibid., 31.
[7]   *Innovation and Entrepreneurship*, 118.
[8]   Ibid., 120.

What is obvious is that innovation is *not* risk-focused. "The popular picture of innovators—half pop-psychology, half Hollywood— makes them look like a cross between Superman and the Knights of the Round Table. Alas, most of them in real life are unromantic figures, and much more likely to spend hours on a cash-flow projection than to dash off looking for 'risks'."[9] Successful innovators, so Drucker stated, are conservative. They have to be. They are not risk takers; they are opportunity-focused.

Both Schumpeter and Drucker highlighted the importance and role of innovation and entrepreneurship in economic development: the former stressed the dynamic leadership role of the entrepreneur in modern capitalism; the latter outlined the rules of innovation as an entrepreneurial discipline. Neither Schumpeter nor Drucker paid much attention to the role of religion and religious motives in advancing entrepreneurship—at least not in a systematic way. This conclusion also holds true for current studies on entrepreneurship. But these studies, to which we now turn, do provide important insights into how entrepreneurs think, into the different types of entrepreneurs, and into entrepreneurial leadership.

The Entrepreneurial Difference: Seizing Opportunity

In the last twenty-five years, the study of entrepreneurship has developed into a mature branch of scientific research. The work by Schumpeter and Drucker—though to a lesser degree—has been pioneering in this respect. I will not attempt to give a full summary of the main findings, but I will present some conclusions that are directly relevant to the topic of the present study, that is, the peculiar blending of entrepreneurism and the beliefs and values of Calvinist Dutch-American industrialists and businessmen. A conclusion that is already evident is that there is a lack of systematic empirical research into the contemporary (post-Weberian) role of religion in understanding various forms of entrepreneurship. I will come back to this point in the next section.

First of all, *what* is entrepreneurship? The etymological root of the term derives from the French verb "entreprendre," meaning "to undertake, to launch, to begin, to attempt, to contract for, or to adventure." The word *entrepreneur* was first used in the Middle Ages to indicate a person who is active and gets things done. Entrepreneurship is a behavioral characteristic of individuals. It is not an occupation. It does

---

9   Ibid., 127.

not equal starting a small business; it is not the same as management, and it is not restricted to the commercial sector. A comprehensive and useful definition is given by Carree and Thurik: "Entrepreneurship is the manifest ability and willingness of individuals, on their own, in teams, within and outside existing organizations to perceive and create new economic opportunities (new products, new production methods, new organizational schemes and new product-market combinations) and to introduce their ideas in the market, in the face of uncertainty and other obstacles, by making decisions on location, form and the use of resources and institutions."[10]

Although entrepreneurship is not the same as founding a new business, I am, in this study, particularly interested in entrepreneurs who started new and successful ventures—the so-called nascent entrepreneurs.[11] Several researchers have established typologies and taxonomies to classify entrepreneurs. Collins and Moore[12] differentiate between the "administrative entrepreneur" and the "independent entrepreneur." Lafuente and Salas[13] distinguish between the "craft," "risk-oriented," "family-oriented," and "managerial entrepreneur;" and Filion[14] makes a distinction between the "operator" and the "visionary entrepreneur." These typologies vary on the dimensions of management orientation and substantive focus of entrepreneurship. Chell gives a more functional taxonomy: "novice entrepreneurs" (no prior experience of founding a business), "habitual entrepreneurs" (founders that have started several businesses), "serial entrepreneurs" (who found, disengage, and start a further business), and "portfolio entrepreneurs" (who retain, inherit or purchase the business they found).[15]

[10] Martin A. Carree and A. Roy Thurik, "The Impact of Entrepreneurship on Economic Growth," in: Zoltan J. Acs and David B. Audretsch, eds., *Handbook of Entrepreneurship Research. An Interdisciplinary Survey and Introduction* (New York: Springer, 2005 [hardcover edition 2003]), 564.

[11] See William B. Gartner and Nancy M. Carter, "Entrepreneurial Behavior and Firm Organizing Behavior," in: Acs & Audretsch, *Handbook of Entrepreneurship*.

[12] Orvis F. Collins and David G. Moore, *The Organization Makers: A Behavioral Study of Independent Entrepreneurs* (New York: Appleton-Century-Crofts [Meredith Corp.], 1970).

[13] Alberto Lafuente and Vicente Salas, "Types of Entrepreneurs and Firms: The Case of New Spanish Firms," *Strategic Management Journal* 10 (1989): 17-30.

[14] Louis J. Filion, "Two Types of Entrepreneurs: The Operator and the Visionary. Consequences for Education," working paper no. 1998-11; HEC, The University of Montreal Business School, Canada.

[15] Elizabeth Chell, *The Entrepreneurial Personality. A Social Construction*, 2nd ed. (London: Routledge, 2008), 8-10. See also Deniz Ucbasaran, Paul Westhead and Mike Wright, "Habitual Entrepreneurs," in: Mark Casson, Bernard Yeung, Anuradha Basu, and Nigel Wadeson, eds., *The Oxford Handbook of Entrepreneurship* (Oxford: Oxford University Press, 2006), 461-83.

A substantial number of studies have been conducted on "the entrepreneurial personality," that is, the issue of whether entrepreneurs have particular personality traits that distinguish them from non-entrepreneurs. These attempts have not been very successful. Part of the explanation is that the category of entrepreneurs (and for that matter, non-entrepreneurs as well) is quite heterogeneous. They may share the entrepreneurial spirit (idea, vision, or dream), but their personalities may differ markedly. Peter Drucker already pointed this out. There is no single trait that differentiates entrepreneurs from non-entrepreneurs. Traits are at best modalities and not universal features. We have to link entrepreneurial traits to entrepreneurial performance, outcomes, and context. Some psychological traits are necessary but insufficient conditions for successful entrepreneurship.

Three of the earlier traits that have been studied in relationship to entrepreneurship are need for achievement, locus of control, and risk-taking propensity. Intuitively one would assume that entrepreneurship is positively related to achievement motivation, internal locus of control, and the willingness to take risk. Elizabeth Chell, in her comprehensive overview study of the entrepreneurial personality, concluded, however, that empirical evidence for the psychological correlates of entrepreneurship is mixed.[16] Let us take a look at risk-taking propensity. The lay notion here is probably that a successful entrepreneur is a risk taker. But in reality a successful entrepreneur—as Drucker also stated—is a *calculated* risk taker: the perceived benefits of entrepreneurial action are weighted against the probability of success. Entrepreneurs "enjoy the excitement of a challenge, but they don't gamble. Entrepreneurs avoid low-risk situations because there is a lack of challenge, and they avoid high-risk situations because they want to succeed. They like achievable challenges."[17] They dislike entrepreneurial activity that depends on chance rather than on efforts. And maybe they are more optimistic about the outcomes of their efforts than non-entrepreneurs, but that does not make them more risk prone.

But this critical approach of the entrepreneurial personality does not contradict the notion that a certain psychological mindset helps entrepreneurs to be creative, innovative, and successful. Recent studies have come up with more promising cognitive stylistics and heuristics that are related to entrepreneurship. Psychological factors such as opportunity recognition, proactive personality, self-efficacy,

---

[16] Chell, *The Entrepreneurial Personality*, chapter 4.
[17] G. G. Meredith, R. E. Nelson, and P. A. Neck, *The Practice of Entrepreneurship* (Geneva: ILO International Labour Office, 1982), 25.

social competence, and good intuition, turn out to be decisive.[18] A successful entrepreneur sees and creates opportunity for innovation and has sensitivity for good timing. He or she has the convictions and hopes that the opportunity will be realized and is alert and proactive to seize occurring opportunities.[19] Creative entrepreneurs think outside the box; they make the difference, and are convinced of the innovation of their idea and approach. Good intuition, energy, and drive are vital, and so are commitment, determination, and perseverance. Effective entrepreneurs have a sense of self-efficacy and know how to mobilize the necessary resources (for example, financial) and social networks to start their venture. Calculative risk management is central. They must avoid or learn from decision-making errors, cognitive biases, judgment oversights, and overconfidence. Sometimes they benefit from a little creative opportunism. Successful entrepreneurs have the social skills to sell their idea and persuade others for support, and they have the strategic and entrepreneurial skills to exploit their new idea or product, to manage people, and to cope with difficulties. Ultimately, they must be able to grow and sustain the enterprise. A successful entrepreneur, in short, needs the right combination of hard and soft entrepreneurial skills.

[18]   Chell, *The Entrepreneurial Personality*, 247.
[19]   See for the notion of proactive entrepreneurial alertness: C. M. Gaglio and J. A. Katz, "The Psychological Basis of Opportunity Identification: Entrepreneurial Alertness," *Small Business Economics* 16 (2001): 95-11.

CHAPTER 3

Calvinist Entrepreneurs: Challenging Questions

Religion and Entrepreneurship: An Underdeveloped Research Area

The overview in the previous chapter of research findings on correlates of entrepreneurship clearly shows that the religious factor is under-theorized and under-researched.[1] In fact, it hardly plays a role at all in mainstream entrepreneurship theory and research. This holds for both the antecedents and consequences of modern entrepreneurship. Dodd and Gotsis are quite right in their assessment that "religious spaces

---

[1] The study of the relationship between religion, entrepreneurship, and immigration is somewhat of an exception. The role of religion in establishing ethnic entrepreneurship in immigrant cultures in particular has attracted more research attention., e.g., Anuraha Basu, "Ethnic Minority Entrepreneurship," in: Casson et al., *The Oxford Handbook of Entrepreneurship*, 580-600. This is also true for more historical analyses of how religion and ethnicity affect entrepreneurship, e.g. Chris Minns and Marian Rizov, "The Spirit of Capitalism? Ethnicity, Religion, and Self-employment in Early 20th Century Canada," in *Explorations in Economic History* 42 (2005): 259-81. A second exception is the influence of religion on business ethics. See, e.g., J. Angelidis and N. Ibrahim, "An Exploratory Study of the Impact of Degree of Religiousness upon an Individual's Corporate Social Responsiveness Orientation," in *Journal of Business Ethics* 51 (2004): 118-28.

and discourses are ... rarely privileged in the study of entrepreneurship, in spite of their social and symbolic power."[2] A close look at three of the most reputed recent handbooks on entrepreneurship,[3] substantiates the observation that studying the religious factor is not a prominent topic on the entrepreneurship research agenda. A first attempt at systematizing some findings by Dodd and Gotsis indicates that the relationships between entrepreneurship and religion are dependent on context and vary over time and social setting, mediated by political institutions and ideologies. Religion appears to have an impact on the entrepreneur's belief matrix, which in turn may affect his decision-making by setting specific criteria upon which decisions are made. It must be added, however, that most of the studies cited by Dodd and Gotsis used samples of students and managers, and did not use interviews of highly successful, top-level entrepreneurs. This focus on general non-CEO samples—particularly students—is typical for mainstream research on religion and business ethics, beliefs, and attitudes.[4]

At the macro level—the level of societies and cultures—there is some evidence of a relationship between cultural characteristics and entrepreneurship, particularly along the line of Hofstede's well-known cultural dimensions (individualism/collectivism, power distance, uncertainty, avoidance, masculinity/femininity, and long versus short-term orientation).[5] Cultures that value high individualism, high masculinity, low uncertainty avoidance, and low power distance are conducive to entrepreneurship.[6] Furthermore, there is cross-cultural research that shows that national cultures that are based on

---

[2]   Sarah Drakopoulou Dodd and George Gotsis, "The Interrelationships between Entrepreneurship and Religion," *Entrepreneurship and Innovation* 8 (2007): 93. See also Sarah Drakopoulou Dodd and Paul.T. Seaman, *"Religion and Enterprise: An Introductory Exploration,"* *Entrepreneurship Theory & Practice* 23 (1998): 71-86.

[3]   Casson et al., *The Oxford Handbook of Entrepreneurship*; Acs, and Audretsch, eds., *Handbook of Entrepreneurial Research*; Chell, *The Entrepreneurial Personality*.

[4]   Cf. Corrie Mazereeuw-van der Duijn Schouten, *Doing Business for Heaven's Sake: Studies on the Relationship between Religiosity and Socially Responsible Business Conduct*, PhD Thesis (Tilburg: Tilburg University, 2010). G. R. Weaver and B. R. Angle, "Religiosity and Ethical Behavior in Organizations: A Symbolic Interactionist Perspective," *Academy of Management Review* 27 (2002): 77-97.

[5]   Geert Hofstede, *Culture's Consequences. Comparing Values, Behaviors. Institutions, and Organizations across Nations*, 2nd ed. (Thousand Oaks: Sage Publications, 2001).

[6]   James Hayton, Gerard George, and Shaker A. Zahra, "National Culture and Entrepreneurship: A Review of Behavioral Research," *Entrepreneurship Theory and Practice* 26 (2002): 22-49. See for a balanced review of these studies: Amir N. Licht and Jordan I. Siegel, "The Social Dimensions of Entrepreneurship," in: Casson et al., *The Oxford Handbook of Entrepreneurship*, 511-39.

predominantly egalitarian religions—such as Protestantism—show higher rates of entrepreneurship; vice versa, if a country's dominant religion is hierarchical—such as Catholicism—lower rates are observed.[7] The values these religions treasure are conducive or unfavorable respective to the development of entrepreneurial ambitions and motivations.[8] But the relationship between national culture and entrepreneurship is a complex one, in which more structural and institutional differences play a role, too.[9] Moreover, nations have become more ethnically and religiously diversified. The monopoly of Protestantism on entrepreneurship has long since disappeared, if it ever was true at all. In a rapidly globalizing world, relationships between religion and entrepreneurship become multifold and complex. This is particularly true for religiously pluralized societies.[10] The symbolic universe has become much more multilateral and diverse. Contemporary culture is colored by a plurality of religious and secular systems of meaning that all—directly or indirectly—have an impact on entrepreneurs and entrepreneurship. And last but not least, one has to be careful to avoid a "fallacy of the wrong level," that is, the role of religion at the macro (societal) level should not be confused with the role played by religion at the micro (individual) level.

For the present study, the lack of systematic research into the relationship between religion and entrepreneurship is both a handicap

---

[7] Recently, some very interesting works have been published on Catholic thought on entrepreneurship. A prime example is: Jeffrey Cornwall and Michael Naughton, *Bringing Your Business to Life. The Four Virtues That Will Help You Build a Better Business and a Better Life* (Ventura, CA: Gospel Lights, 2008). See also their article: "Who is the Good Entrepreneur? An Exploration within the Catholic Social Tradition, *Journal of Business Ethics* 44 (2003): 61-78. Cornwall and Naughton explicitly state that entrepreneurship in Catholic thought—particularly the notions of "virtue" and "courage"—holds significant promise in fostering the common good "as long as entrepreneurs see their work not only in terms of material gain or technical skill but also in terms of virtue, the common good and a participation in God's creative and redemptive activity,"; Michal J. Naughton and Jeffrey R. Cornwall, "The Virtue of Courage in Entrepreneurship: Engaging the Catholic Social Tradition and the Life-Cycle of the Business," *Business Ethics Quarterly* 47 (2006): 4.

[8] Kathy Fogel, Ashton Hawk, Randall Morck and Bernard Yeung, "Institutional Obstacles to Entrepreneurship," in: Casson et al., *The Oxford Handbook of Entrepreneurship*, 540-79.

[9] Mazereeuw-van der Duijn Schouten, *Doing Business for Heaven's Sake*, 19.

[10] An interesting case here is New Zealand. In their study on attitudes toward entrepreneurship, Carswell and Rolland found that "People of Eastern-based religions are just as likely to believe in the importance of entrepreneurship as people of a Christian perspective." Peter Carswell and Deborah Rolland, "Religion and Entrepreneurship in New Zealand," in *Journal of Enterprising Communities* 1 (2007): 174.

and a challenge. It is a handicap, in the sense that there is no established tradition of research on this topic on which this study can build; this is a challenge, since it evokes the necessity of exploring new research paths.

Main Research Issue: The Linkage between Reformed Faith, Dutch Heritage, and Entrepreneurial Success

The main question this study addresses is whether or not successful Calvinist Dutch-American entrepreneurs relate their achievements to their Calvinist world view, values, and upbringing. Did these three pillars of Calvinist thought contribute to their success as entrepreneurs? or do they believe that their disposition is just part of how their generation of Americans was socialized, apart from religion and ethnicity? How do they define entrepreneurial success? Is it strictly financial? or in a broader sense, is it about making a contribution to the community and to society? Do they believe that personal wealth and societal responsibility are embedded in the Calvinist legacy?

Calvinist upbringing is a key explanatory factor in the way some Dutch-American entrepreneurs view the world—including the world of business—the opportunities it offers and the talents it requires.[11] Let me turn again to Amway's co-founder, Dutch-American Rich DeVos—a lifelong member of the Christian Reformed Church—who explicitly relates his Calvinist rearing to what he coined "compassionate capitalism" and his entrepreneurial values:

> When I was a child growing up in Grand Rapids, Michigan, every Sunday my mother would cook the family breakfast and head us toward the door. 'Sunday is God's day,' she would remind anyone not in the mood for Sunday school or church. 'And like it or not, we're going to be there in the front row together.' I didn't have any idea what was happening to me during those early childhood years, and there were times I resisted that Sunday morning tradition with all my young heart and soul. But although I won

---

[11]   Cf. Michael Lozon, *Mr. Turkey: A Biography of Bil Mar Foods Co-Founder, Marvin DeWitt* (Zeeland: The DeWitt Foundation, 1999); Larry Mulder, *The Morning. A Narrative History of ODL, Incorporated. The First Fifty Years: 1945-1995* (Zeeland: ODL, 2003); Michael Lozon, *The Sun Never Sets on Big Dutchman. From Farm Boys to International Businessmen – How Jack and Dick DeWitt Transformed a Tiny Hatchery into a World-Wide Supplier of Automatic Poultry Equipment* (Jack DeWitt Family, Zeeland, MI, 2004). Michal Lozon, *Sharing the Wealth. The Biography of a Cheerful Giver: Automotive Entrepreneur and Philanthropist Peter C. Cook* (Grand Rapids: Cook Holdings LLC., 2007).

an occasional battle, Mom won the war. Rain or shine, snow or hail, the DeVos family went to church. And during those Sunday school lessons, hymns, and sermons that seemed to go on forever, a seed was planted in me that would permanently change my life. My parents and that long list of pastors, teachers, deacons, and lay volunteers whose names I can't even remember were passing on to me life's greatest gift: a road map to follow on my journey and a source of strength and comfort on the way. Thanks to my mother, my value system is based on the Christian tradition.[12]

This value system, centered on very basic Calvinist doctrines that Dutch immigrants brought with them from the Old Country, is in many respects characteristic for the DeVos generation of Dutch-Americans. It is evident from a study I recently completed on the formative experiences and youth memories of older Dutch-Americans living in the Holland, Michigan area, that being raised in a strict Calvinist Dutch-American environment had a lasting influence on this generation.[13] This generation clearly indicated that their upbringing was dominated by uncompromising Calvinist norms, values, and regulations. Key features of their Dutch-American (Christian) Reformed socialization were strong religious beliefs and norms, a determined Christian life style, resolute church involvement, rigid Sunday observance, pronounced work ethic, and firm family values. Some originally Dutch settlements intentionally market the economic benefits of their solid Dutch background and solid values. Here is how the chamber of commerce in Zeeland, Michigan subtly portrays its community:

> "Zeeland is a beautiful area that shows pride in its historical background and its strong religious heritage. The city, named after the Province of Zeeland in the Netherlands, was settled in 1847 by a group of 457 courageous settlers who were seeking religious and political freedom.... A strong work ethic is evident in the quality work force in the area, and pride is apparent in the upkeep of homes and businesses."[14]

---

[12]   DeVos, *Compassionate Capitalism*, 55.
[13]   Peter Ester, "'It was very, very churchy.' Recollections of Older Dutch-Americans on Growing Up in Holland, Michigan," *Oral History Review* 35 (2008): 117-38.
[14]   See: http//www.zeelandcofc.org. For an interesting analysis of how the Protestant work ethic operates in the Zeeland community, see the MA thesis of Emma de Ruiter, "People, Product, Progress" (in Dutch) [A study on the work ethic in Zeeland, West Michigan, founded by a group of Calvinist emigrants in 1847] (University of Amsterdam, 1999).

Jay Van Andel, business partner of Rich DeVos and one of the most successful Dutch-American entrepreneurs, explicitly states a straightforward relationship between his upbringing in the Reformed faith and his business values: "Two basic distinctives of Reformed churches were the emphasis on the sovereignty of God and the responsibility of man to live faithfully by God's word in every part of life, and as I look back I'd have to say that all my political, economic, and entrepreneurial beliefs come from these two tenets of my religious upbringing."[15] Being raised in the Reformed way of thinking and entrepreneurial beliefs are—so the hypothesis runs—like intertwined strands of cultural DNA. In this study I will make an attempt to test this intriguing hypothesis.

---

[15]   Van Andel, *An Enterprising Life*, 2-3. He furthermore states in an almost Weberian fashion that "from my Calvinist heritage, I learned that our work is done in the context of a calling, which assures us that, no matter what our income level, education, or family background, we each are equal in our ability to glorify God in our work," 20.

PART II

METHODOLOGY

CHAPTER 4

Methods: Interviewing Outstanding Dutch-American Entrepreneurs

CEO Sample and Interviews

My main research questions can be summarized as follows:

1. Do highly successful Calvinist entrepreneurs with a Dutch-American background relate their business achievements to their Dutch-American upbringing and Calvinist beliefs and values?

2. If so, is the impact of ethnicity and religion a direct or indirect one? Is ethnicity more important than religion or vice versa?

3. If so, what are the main characteristics of their upbringing and religious perspective that they link to their success in business?

4. How do successful Dutch-American entrepreneurs define their success, and how do they perceive their role in society?

As indicated above, the scarce studies that have been done on the relationship between religion and entrepreneurship typically used student samples or managers. Systematic studies among samples of highly successful entrepreneurs and their religious beliefs are hard to find. In this study I intend to fill this gap. By focusing on West Michigan entrepreneurs with a Calvinist Dutch-American background, I intend to reach three goals simultaneously:

1. Sample highly successful entrepreneurs (focus on entrepreneurs who made it)

2. Study the perceived impact of a Calvinist worldview and Calvinist upbringing on entrepreneurship (focus on a specific religious tradition)

3. Minimize external heterogeneity (focus on West Michigan)

I fully realize that this approach raises methodological issues. First of all, non-successful entrepreneurs are not included. Although this is on purpose, it may well generate self-selectivity effects, that is, a Calvinist upbringing and world view may have a differential impact on successful and failing entrepreneurs. Second, it remains unclear whether observed findings are to be generalized to other ethnic groups of Protestants. Third, we do not know how effects hold for other religious and non-religious entrepreneurs, both in western Michigan and in other regions. A focus on group homogeneity, in short, reduces variance. But this, at least for the moment, is a price I am willing to pay to accomplish the three basic goals guiding this study concurrently. There were also constraints of time and budget.

With the help of a number of professors on the staff of the Van Raalte Institute at Hope College, Holland, Michigan and Calvin College, Grand Rapids, Michigan, and other local and regional experts, a short-list of about two dozen greatly successful Michigan based Dutch-American entrepreneurs was made. Criteria included: the entrepreneurs should be of Dutch descent, founders and/or CEOs or board members of highly successful enterprises (in terms of annual sales, profits, and visibility), and active members of the Reformed Church of America (RCA) or Christian Reformed Church (CRC), both originally "Dutch" Calvinist churches.[1] In May 2010 these entrepreneurs received a letter from the Van Raalte Institute explaining the goal of the study, introducing me as the principal researcher, and asking them to participate in a personal interview with me. Later that month, respondents were contacted to

---

[1]   In one instance, however, both the past and present CEOs of a major corporation do not share a Reformed background. Their business, however, is a prime example of highly successful Dutch-American entrepreneurship. They function as an interesting non-Reformed case in this study of Reformed entrepreneurs.

verify their willingness to participate and, if willing, to set a date and time in the month of July for a face-to-face interview. Twenty-one entrepreneurs accepted the invitation, which was a decidedly satisfying outcome.

The following types of Dutch-American entrepreneurs were interviewed:

- Four (4) founders and CEOs of food service companies, in either food or beverage industries
- Two (2) founders and CEOs of construction companies
- Both a former president and the current chairman of a global enterprise based in West Michigan
- Founder and chairman of multiple enterprises
- President and CEO of a company in the petroleum industry
- Founder and former CEO of a company in the service industry
- Several current or former CEOs in the field of automation, transportation and logistics
- Both the former and current CEO of a major regional merchandiser
- Four (4) former CEOs, presidents and chairs of several different international manufacturing companies located in West Michigan, specializing in products for the automotive, construction or furniture industry
- Several of these individuals currently preside over capital management companies or charitable foundations

This impressive list of participating entrepreneurs represents the most successful Dutch-American entrepreneurs and enterprises in West Michigan with an impact and markets that extend well beyond the state level and often even involve global economic activities. Most entrepreneurs know each other well.

The interviews were all conducted face-to-face, by me alone, and were taped with a digital recorder.[2] Interviews were conducted between 5 July and 30 July 2010, either at the respondent's home or

---

[2] Full transcripts were made of each interview, using Express Scribe software recommended by the British Library Sound Archive (http://www.bl.uk/nsa). Many thanks to Rob Perks, Oral History Department, British Library for his practical suggestions. Of course, I asked respondents for their permission to tape the interview. None of them objected.

office or at the Van Raalte Institute. I will not use respondents' real names but pseudonyms in order to assure their anonymity and privacy. Confidentiality of the interviews will, of course, be respected. As a rule I will quote respondents literally, and will not change their wording, style, or grammar.

The questionnaire, included in the appendix, is centered on the following themes:

- Respondent's personal characteristics and demographics (age, church affiliation, family members involved in the company)
- Saliency of Dutch background, pride of Dutch heritage
- Upbringing: values, beliefs, norms, non-negotiable matters, strictness, basis for later entrepreneurial career
- Youth years and the church: Sunday observance, role of church, rules and obligations
- Entrepreneurship: qualities of successful entrepreneurs, perceived impact of respondent's upbringing, examples of impact, company values, common features of successful Dutch-American entrepreneurs
- Role in society: involvement in civic affairs, community giving, philanthropy and charity, political beliefs, and values

The in-depth interviews, without exception, were very pleasant. Respondents evidently liked to talk about their youth years, their Dutch-American upbringing, and to reflect on how the Calvinist values and beliefs they were taught affected their later entrepreneurial success. Invariably, respondents all granted me more time for the interview then I initially asked for. The average duration of the interviews was about ninety minutes; in some cases interviews lasted two hours. Respondents were remarkably open about their life as a highly successful entrepreneur, their role in society and community affairs, as well as their often very substantial philanthropic contributions.[3] Of course, many of the entrepreneurs with whom I talked, are well experienced in giving interviews about their company. The difference was, as several of my respondents indicated, that they now had to talk about themselves, their upbringing, and their personal Christian beliefs and values. It was a difference that matters.

---

[3]   All interviews were between the interviewee and myself. No participant brought in their company's PR officer. In two cases of home interviews, the respondent's wife was present.

The Personal Interview as Oral History

The methodology used in this study is partly an exercise in oral history. In letting entrepreneurs tell their life history, I attempt to reconstruct the ways their formative years, their Reformed upbringing, and their later business career are interlinked. It is the appropriate method to understand how people look back at their life course, and the major events and transitions that took place.[4] Storytelling is the approach through which respondents make sense of their personal history and career, which unfolds itself within the wider societal context of the formation and life course of their generation.[5]

The role of memory is important. Obviously, people cannot remember all the events and transitions in their childhood and youth years that are related to their Dutch-American Reformed upbringing and their later business success. There is always choice, subjectivity, and bias. In this study, however, I am not interested in the perfect accuracy of respondents' memory, but in the kind of stories they tell about their Dutch-American background, their formative years, and how this relates to their later career as a highly successful entrepreneur. Oral history and its narrative methodology are about subjective significance and not about objective precision.

Doing oral history also has implications for the role of the interviewer. He or she needs to show a keen interest in the stories told by the respondent, not to debate or discuss, but to ask in order to get the story behind the story. To achieve this, one needs the right combination of empathy, sensitivity, and subtlety. If the researcher succeeds in doing so, fascinating and sometimes amazing stories will be the result. Listening to people's life stories is one of the most rewarding professional experiences for the social scientist. This is certainly true for these interviews of highly successful entrepreneurs.

---

[4]   See, e.g., Paul Thompson, *The voice of the past: Oral history*, 3rd ed. (Oxford/New York: Oxford University Press, 2000); Valerie Raleigh Yow, *Recording oral history: A guide for the humanities and social sciences*, 2nd ed. (Walnut Creek, CA: Alta Mira Press, 2005); Donald A. Ritchie, *Doing oral history: A practical guide*, 2nd ed. (London/New York: Oxford University Press, 2003).

[5]   Cf. Ester, "It was very, very churchy."

PART III

Results

CHAPTER 5

Youth Years of Dutch-American Entrepreneurs

Proud Of Dutch Heritage?

A major dimension of immigrants' shared ethnic heritage is a basic sense of pride of one's old country, that is, a prime affection for the family's country of origin, its history and culture, and often for its particular achievements. Being proud of one's ethnic heritage can be seen as a positive effect of the way people identify with their ethnic background. Appreciating one's cultural ancestry is a significant factor in how people connect to their ethnic group. This attachment will vary among immigrants, and its strength is typically related to length of immigrant generation history. The longer one's immigration history, the more symbolic one's ethnic identification and affinity is with the emigration country.[1] How do highly successful Dutch-American

---

[1] Peter Ester, *Growing Up Dutch-American: Ethnic Identity and the Formative Years of the Older Generation of Dutch-Americans* (Holland, MI: Van Raalte Press, 2008). Herbert Gans, "Symbolic Ethnicity: The Future of Ethnic Groups and Cultures in America," in *Theories of Ethnicity: A Classical Reader*, ed. Werner Sollors (New York: New York University Press, 1996), 436. First published in *On the Making of Americans: Essays in Honor of David Riesman*, ed. Herbert J. Gans (Philadelphia: University of Pennsylvania Press, 1979).

CEOs feel about their Dutch descent? Is having a Dutch background important and meaningful to them? Or do they view their Dutch heritage with a combination of indifference and irrelevance?

Inspection of the data reveals three groups: the first and by far the largest group expressed a basic and strong affinity with its Dutch descent. A second and much smaller group conditioned its pride of their Dutch background, and a third almost negligibly small group was simply indifferent about its heritage. Here are some examples of the first group of CEOs that cherish its Dutch ancestry and descent: "Absolutely, on the census forms I check the 'Other' box and write in *Dutch*." (Adrian D.).[2] "Yes, the short answer to that is that I am proud of my Dutch heritage, and I have been all my life . . . I thank God I am Dutch, and I thank God that someone else is African. I don't have any problems with other ethnicities. I am just glad I know where I am from." (Mike V.). "I am very proud and thankful for my heritage." (Gene H.). "I am extremely proud of it. They were great people the Dutchmen, and that's the long and short of it." (Thomas V.). The second group explicitly prioritized being American over being of Dutch descent. They are certainly proud of their Dutch background but as one respondent argued, they are Americans of Dutch descent not Dutch Americans: "Proud of our tradition? Absolutely, but we are *Americans* who are proud of our Dutch background . . . Our Dutchness is beneath our American-ness." (Dale Z.). And there is the generational argument: "My grandfather was born in the Netherlands, so I'm kind of now third generation. I think the further generations you get away, the further you get away from the Dutch heritage." (Chris G.). There is only one example of a Dutch-American entrepreneur for whom his ethnic heritage is not important, but his twist to the argument is quite interesting: "I've got no affinity for the Netherlands whatsoever. I don't identify myself with the Netherlands—I identify myself with the Reformed, but not Dutch Reformed." (Mark F.). In this case religion overrides ethnicity as the prime source of identification.

What are the main ingredients of CEOs' affinity with their Dutch background? Shared values and Dutch history feature prominently among positive ethnic identification. "The Dutch were tremendous innovators, whether conscious or not, and brought that mind set, and that mind set is very much part of the business community here, that mindset of innovation and making your future type of thing." (Harry

---

[2]   Respondents' names in this section are all made up, but the quotations are exclusively drawn from the interviews themselves. Last names given by the author have been reduced to the first letter.—Ed.

V.). "I think throughout the world the Dutch have a great reputation of being fair-minded; they are inquisitive; they're travelers, and they tend to behave themselves. They know how to conduct themselves in social settings. They tend to be the ones that take responsibility. If you look at what the Dutch have made of what was a lot of swamp . . . there's something genetically that drives us. The Dutch people tend to be successful." (Adrian D.). "There's just so many things that Holland had an influence on way beyond other countries." (Thomas D.). "When you look back and you put into perspective what the Dutch have accomplished given the size of their population . . . it appears to me there is a wonderful tradition of entrepreneurship in the Netherlands, going back centuries. . . . I grew up in Holland, Michigan and there is a strong affinity to the Dutch heritage; the ties with the Netherlands have lasted substantially longer and uniquely stronger than among many other immigrant groups. I would speculate this has to do with that they came over here to practice their particular religious beliefs and they wanted to be a group of people apart." (Jerry V.). "A Dutch heritage implies this Protestant work ethic, frugality, hard work, a commitment to community, commitment to family, all characteristics that in my mind are very, very healthy." (Luke Z.). "I am proud because I think I have been brought up in a way to appreciate integrity and honesty and values and faith, and so when I look at my heritage—now I am not one that goes and researches in a library—but when I look at my grandparents and my parents, I am very proud and pleased that I came from that kind of background." (Peter B.). "I think the Netherlands is a magnificent country. It's not a great piece of real estate—half of it was underwater, right? And just what's been done with that they can teach the world about water management. A great port in Rotterdam, great companies. For a small country as it is, it has dominated the world in history—the old Dutch-East Indies company centuries ago. It's fascinating." (David S.). But it is not all roses in the Netherlands. "I felt prouder of it many years ago. When the Netherlands' culture and moral values went down, I didn't feel as good about my Dutch heritage as what I used to." (Albert I.) And—in the same vein—"the Netherlands is going to the left, it is too liberal, freedoms are being disguised as anything goes." (James M.).

It can be concluded that the vast majority of successful Dutch-American CEOs have a (very) positive feeling about their ethnic heritage, a feeling that is determined by three factors in particular: their family emigrated from the Netherlands, Dutch-American culture is about important religious, personal, and social values, and the Netherlands has a peculiar history of achievement and impact.

Upbringing and Values

A key assumption of this study is that the Reformed upbringing of Dutch-American entrepreneurs and the values they were taught in their formative years were a good (direct or indirect) basis for their later success in business. But what were the principles and standards that guided their upbringing? What were the rules, norms, and ethics which their parents and the church emphasized when these future CEOs were growing up? Do they cherish their youth memories? or do they feel that their childhood socialization was too strict and restrictive? Findings indicate that there was a strong impact of Reformed thought and morals during these entrepreneurs' youth, with some variation according to generation and milieu. Results also show that the religious element in their upbringing was more important than their ethnic background.

Reformed principles and morals penetrated all domains of life and guided one's way of thinking. "There was a sense of responsibility. We were expected to think things through and do our chores, take responsibility for what you do." (Adrian D.). "The Reformed theology permeated our lifestyle. . . . Number one is the sense that what I have is not mine, I have been entrusted with it, but it belongs, both the talent and the resources, to God. . . . The second one is it gives you a long term viewpoint, that viewpoint being that what you do is not necessarily just for today and tomorrow, it is for next year, the next generation, and perhaps for eternity." (Jerry V.). "God was the center of our existence. Relying on God. I was taught to work hard. I always had a job at home, as a little kid. I also was an entrepreneurial person when I was a kid. Picking asparagus, making it into bundles, and going up and down the street selling asparagus for 10 cents a bundle. I had jobs all from the time I was ten on. I enjoyed having jobs." (Mike V.). "Disciplined, I would say disciplined. I knew what the rules were. There were certain things I was supposed to do. My task was to sweep the driveways. There were things like that. . . . It was a Christian-based culture, a value-based culture. God was the center of our lives, we had a conscientious culture." (Peter B.). "Well, we followed quite closely the teachings of our churches. Church was a huge part of how we grew up and those values were the ones that were transferred to the family. Status wasn't critical, wasn't important, but the integrity of the people was" (Mark F.). "Right off the top of my head: loyalty, hard work, integrity, those were the main values." (Henry W.); "Basically you got an upper on life, you have to work hard." (Arthur N.) "There were certain things that you had to do every week. Whether it was school or chores or Sunday school, you had all those things you had to do. You had a lot of free time, but it was only an allotted, measured free time. You may not do anything beyond that or outside of this allotted time. There were clear rules." (Chris G.). "I had a paper route and it was a wonderful experience, every month I would go collect for the month's delivery of papers. No matter what happened you had a paper at the door, and it was there by five o'clock, and maybe that's where my entrepreneurship began." (Jerry V.). "We understood work . . . neatness, cleanness, be on time, the structure was always be prompt, be clean, look good, dress well. Be on time, yes, and finish, finish, finish." (Robert H.). Daily religious routines were important. "To pause before a meal to pray is just what we have always done as a reminder of thankfulness, a reminder of God's goodness." (Dale Z.). "We always prayed before we ate; we read the Bible, prayed after dinner." (Albert I.). Several respondents point at the significance of tithing—the Old Testament concept of giving ten percent of your earnings to the temple: "Tithing, giving to the church, you did that automatically. It was very much part of our culture." (James M.). "A main value that they taught us as far as from the church and the Christian faith." (Victor H.). "Tithing is huge here; it involved the idea of sharing your blessing back into the community." (Harry V.).

It is evident that the Reformed values and teachings were overpowering influences during the CEOs' formative period. Reformed doctrines and morals taught them responsibility, structure, rules, obedience, hard work, and sharing. God was simply omnipresent.

Do Dutch-American CEOs believe that the values they were brought up with were "typically" Dutch or part of the broader American culture of that time? or are these difficult to disentangle? In other words: are Dutch-Americans different? Here are their answers: "The Dutch are terrific workers. I would match this work force in West Michigan with any workforce in the . . . in the world. They know how to work, they understand it." (Mark F.). "I think the truth is known, if you can get a survey in the state of Michigan of different religious people, how they have prospered, you would know that the Dutchman—it's hard to beat them." (Victor H.). "The Dutch worked harder." (John K.). "I grew up in an upper-middle class neighborhood, and I am struck thinking back on it how many entrepreneurs or small business owners lived on our street. There is a correlation with the Dutch experience, but there are also other things with this community in western Michigan which made it a good place to be an entrepreneur." (Rick P.). "I think the Dutch definitely bring in extra. The Dutch were more inclined—from a labor organizing point of view—to have their own labor associations that didn't believe in strikes. To the extent that they stayed out of the mainstream national movement they were even entrepreneurial on the labor side." (Rick P.). "I think probably a little bit of both. We were raised by the greatest generation. They had endured the Depression; they won World War Two. But I also think there is an aspect of Calvinism which may be a genetic part to being Dutch: the social redemption aspect. It seems that there was always an expectation that you at least met expectations or [even] exceed them." (Adrian D.). "Those values and traditions when I grew up, I thought everyone was Dutch, everyone went to church, all of our neighbors, and respected Sunday as the Sabbath day." (Albert I.). "At the time I was growing up, we were a much more dominantly faith-based community, so I believe that many of the values I grew up with were quite commonplace in our society. But I believe that they were much more important and more strongly advocated in this West Michigan Dutch Calvinist society." (Jerry V.). "They [the Dutch] pick up but they won't quit. That is what I have learned under Dutch heritage. Now that doesn't mean Italians or Germans do not have a different way of going about it. But me, I have really learned to respect that they are concerned about finishing what you started, in church, in the people you work with, in your business." (Robert H.). "The emphasis on the entrepreneurial, the emphasis on being diligent, being a good steward of what God has given you, that was uniquely Reformed Dutch." (Mike V.). "I don't know that I would necessarily tie it to being Dutch-American. I'd tie that more to the Calvinist values, kind of almost on that side of the equation. But a lot of those values translate around the world in other cultures and religions." (Chris G.).

Reformed beliefs and values had more determiniation in their family life than did their Dutch descent. "My parents never talked about being Dutch, my parents talked about work, catechism, Sunday school, and education." (Albert I.). "We are Dutch but we don't identify strongly as being that." (Mark F.). "The Dutch language was never transmitted in my family. My wife and I come from 100 percent Dutch extraction, and in both our families our grandparents would speak some Dutch but never taught it to our parents and it never translated to us." (Dale Z.). "Dutch American: it doesn't really impact what I do."(Mark F.). "I am very proud of my Dutch descent but it's because of the Christian values that make me proud of my upbringing." (Gene H.). "I don't necessarily pull Calvinist values and Dutch heritage together. I keep them a little bit separate. A lot of it to me is more Calvinist values than Dutch upbringing that molded who I am." (Chris G.).

We may conclude from these responses that some of the features that characterized the upbringing of CEOs were more related to the

Reformed part than to the ethnic part of their Dutch-American identity. Faith was far more important than ethnicity. But in reality, of course, being Dutch-American almost by definition implied being Reformed or Christian Reformed. The religious and ethnic dimensions are nearly inseparable in view of the peculiar immigration history of the Dutch in West Michigan. Hans Krabbendam points at an interesting cultural paradox in this context: the stronger the religious identity of an immigrant group, the less it needs an explicit national or ethnic identity.[3] The Dutch roots of Dutch-American CEOs help to explain their historic origin, but their Reformed faith, religion, and churches justify and reinforce their cultural identity and existential consciousness.[4]

Next to one's family, the school was a major social institution that taught basic values and norms. For many Reformed—especially Christian Reformed—Dutch-American families, Christian schools were seen as an essential pillar of their communities in guaranteeing orthodox Calvinist teachings, Reformed values, Bible knowledge, good citizenship, and in securing the chain of the three dominant Reformed links: home, church, and school. Christian schools were seen as "the feeders of the church."[5] But Christian schools, compared to public schools were expensive: tuition fees were stiff for ordinary households. For many CRC but also RCA members, attending Christian schools was imperative and they were willing—literally—to pay the price. "The Dutch here put a premium on education." (Rick P.). Christian schools were costly, and for the parents of many of these CEOs, this required considerable sacrifice. "We would save waste paper, newspapers, cardboard boxes. We would put it in the one stall garage that we had at that time, we would fill it all up, and then the semi truck would come and haul it all away, and my mother would get a check in the mail, and that would go toward the payment of my Christian education." (Gene H.). The effects of attending Christian school lasted a lifetime. "As I look back now, most of the relationships I have with men my age, relationships of long standing, virtually all of them went to the Christian school." (Dale Z.).

Do Dutch-American CEOs characterize their upbringing as rather strict or as more lenient? Results show some variety, but in most cases, there were clear boundaries which over the decades tended

---

[3]   Krabbendam, *Freedom on the Horizon*, 333.
[4]   The same pattern was found in my study, *Growing up Dutch-American*.
[5]   Robert P. Swierenga, *Dutch Chicago: A History of the Hollanders in the Windy City* (Grand Rapids: Eerdmans, 2002), chapter 7.

to become somewhat more flexible. As one CEO nicely states: "We had a generous road but clear edges." (Dale Z.). Clear rules typified the formative period of most Dutch-American CEOs on which the Reformed faith and tradition had a major influence. "I would not say super strict but certainly not lenient. Strong expectations in terms of how I should behave." (Harry V.) "I would call it disciplined, and I knew what the rules were." (Peter B.). "The Ten Commandments. Sunday, every Sunday we went to church." (Dale Z.). "Very, very strict, I had problems with that." (Matt H.). "Strict. Yeah, it was strict. Looking back it was all about control; where you were, what you were doing, what time you'd be home, where you were going." (Robert H.). "I'd say: strict by the world's standards, but for our world, the world was pretty much the church, the Christian Reformed Church." (Jeff C.). "Very strict. I couldn't ride a bicycle on Sunday" (David S.). But for other Dutch CEOs, there was also a degree of self-direction and tolerance. "I never found my parents strict, but that's a relative term. They were not inflexible or intolerant." (Jerry V.). "In a way I was raised liberally and in another way, I think, by very strict standards. The liberal part would be to challenge conventional wisdom." (Thomas D.).

What were the issues that were absolutely non-negotiable matters when Reformed Dutch-American entrepreneurs were young? What were behaviors that were not tolerated? "Honesty and integrity were absolutely essential." (Dale Z.). "There was never a doubt that we were going to church on Sunday." (Adrian D.). "We had to go to church, twice on Sunday, and catechism Saturday morning and later Wednesday night." (Albert I.). "Had to go to church. I was brought up in a time you didn't ride your bike on Sunday. And to this day I don't approve of the kids water skiing on Sunday." (Peter B.). "Absolutely non-negotiable is to treat your mother with utmost respect and no tolerance for any kind of disrespect for your mother." (Adrian D.). "We did not have a lot of legislative prescribed rules. There was just this expectation of responsibility." (Luke Z.). This issue of cultural no-go areas also raised some painful memories. "Well, you were never explained what was right or wrong. There was no communication. I felt very insecure." (Robert H.). "One of the disadvantages of my background is that God was in a box. I mean you worshipped him at ten o'clock on Sunday, you worshiped him at seven o'clock at night. You can do some things in the middle, but you better not go over the line or else you are going to hell. And that's not where God is at all. God is real and intimate." (Mike V.).

It is obvious from these examples that matters that were not subject to discussion or negotiation were related especially to Sunday observance; going to church was non-negotiable in Reformed families. This observation leads to a more in-depth analysis of the role of the Reformed and Christian Reformed Churches when Dutch-American CEOs were growing up.

Formative Period and the Church

Church, obviously, was the overarching social institution during the youth years of this generation of Dutch-American entrepreneurs. The church—Reformed and Christian Reformed—provided identity, cohesion, and solidarity. It offered meaning, comfort, and structure. The church prescribed rules of conduct, rituals, and values, exercised social control and authority, and regulated the relationships with the non-Reformed world. The church pervaded all domains of life. It was *the* dominant institution. How do Dutch-American CEOs look back at the role of the church during their formative years, the rules and norms they were supposed to obey, the Sabbath practices they needed to observe, and the strictness of the doctrines that were at the heart of the Reformed faith and tradition? Do they believe that observances were generally too harsh, or were those feelings simply non-existent? Did they bend the rules? The role of the church and the Reformed "do's and don'ts" in their youth were favorite subjects to our sample of outstanding entrepreneurs, to which they easily related, and which prompted many spontaneous reminiscences. This was clearly *their* subject, of which they have vivid memories, and about which they could effortlessly express their views. The memory lane of Dutch-American CEOs is definitely paved with church-related stories. Church was (and to a large extent still is) the most significant force as these Dutch-American entrepreneurs grew up.

Sunday was the most important day of the week, and Sunday observance was—as we saw—a crucial and non-negotiable topic, among both Reformed and Christian Reformed families. Being flexible with observing the Sabbath was a big taboo. You had to go to church, and, on Sunday, as a rule, you had to go twice. "There was a discipline about Sunday that first of all, you don't make me wake you up for church, because you know what time it is, how long it takes you to get ready. There was this kind of expectation, there was some strictness." (Peter B.). "Everything was about discipline. We are leaving at quarter of nine, be ready, and your hair had to be brushed, combed, your clothes had to be pressed. Everything was about how you looked, clean and neat, be there well ahead of time, you would sit in the same place, you listen to the sermon. You would go outside where everyone had a cigarette; that was part of the Christian Reformed experience. It was hard for me to understand as a kid. Part of the Bible you talk about health, you had to refrain from all those things." (Robert H.). "As a child I hated Sundays. I didn't understand a lot of it. I'd be a kid sitting in the bench, and a pastor talking about the Heidelberg Catechism. I didn't understand that Heidelberg was a town in Germany." (David S.). "I will truly say I wasn't bored in church. But I can remember always wondering why the consistory had to sit up front and be separate like that." (James M.) Some of the older Dutch-American CEOs remember that sometimes the service was in Dutch. "I just thought it was a little bit useless. I couldn't understand the sermon, but I could talk to my dad, you know. My dad always prayed in Dutch." (Victor H.).

Though the strictness of Sunday rules somewhat differed between Dutch-American entrepreneurs when they were young, there generally were clear regulations. "The only thing I was really allowed to do on Sunday, other than be in church, was to take walks. So we would go for a walk in downtown Zeeland, and that was not a real exciting place in the early fifties." (Matt H.). "Never did anything on Sunday but read *The Banner*." (Gene H.). "A typical Sunday consisted of church, church in the morning, Sunday school in the morning. A late afternoon youth experience, which was called Christian Endeavor, followed by going to the evening service, more often than I would have liked to. But I would go out with the guys in the afternoons, go for a ride or go for a swim, play golf, that sort of thing." (Jerry V.). "Sundays [you] couldn't do anything. And that was the Dutch Reformed tradition back then. We couldn't ride horse; we had to polish our shoes on Saturday night, peel the potatoes on Saturday night—pretty strict." (Albert I.). "We did go to the beach. Growing up on the lake, that was just a very natural thing to do. Now, having said that, all these little nuances slip in to how you interpret what you do on Sunday; we could take the boat out, but we couldn't go water-skiing." (Peter B.). "It was very interesting rules. I could play hockey, but you didn't put on all the pads. My wife's family . . . she tells stories of being at her uncle's cottage, where you could sit on the dock by the lake and have your feet in, but you couldn't swim." (Jeff C.). "No, we did not have particularly strict guidelines. We could watch Sunday afternoon football but without the sound. I never understood that. I've asked my mother and she said she saw the young generation kind of fading away, and that was her way to grab it. You can kind of enjoy the game, but you're not going to love it." (Dale Z.). "We could ride our bikes, but we couldn't go swimming. But after a while, that rule was more lax." (Mike V.).

The introduction of new technologies raised interesting disputes that called for new rules. Sometimes the adoption of such technologies was frowned upon. Television was an interesting case, also in view of the difference in acceptance speed by CRC and RCA families. "The Christian Reformed kind of hid their aerials in the attic. Ours [respondent is RCA] was on the ground in the front yard. On Monday we had a grocer coming to the house, he said, 'Is that a Reformed aerial set?' Because he was Christian Reformed, and joked, is that a Reformed aerial set in the front yard? Oh yeah, it was all this stuff, you know." (John K.). "We didn't get a television until I was in the fifth grade, and then I couldn't watch it on Sunday. I remember I could watch it other days, but they inspected what I was watching." (David S.).

Shopping and going to restaurants on Sunday is another interesting case because here the world of religious strictness and the world of business met, which often created conflicts. A clear example of this confrontation was the Sunday opening of Meijer's stores in the late sixties. Fred Meijer vividly remembered some of the harsh responses by church people. He recalled receiving many furious letters. "All heck broke loose. It was a tough time, but we weathered it."[6] Sunday shopping and restaurant visits were the exception rather than the rule when CEOs were young. "You were not allowed to go shopping; most of the shops would be closed on Sunday anyway. In fact, where I was brought up there was a department store and they were all Christian Reformed, and they put drapes in front, plain drapes in front of the window, so when you walked by going to church, you couldn't see any merchandise." (Gene H.). "We wouldn't go shopping, and we wouldn't go for lunch or something and pay for lunch." (Jeff C.). "We could never eat in a restaurant on Sunday. Never, never, never." (David S.).

By and large it seems that nowadays most Dutch-American CEOs don't object to going to a restaurant on Sunday, but going shopping is still an issue for many of them. The Sunday brunch after the morning church service is quite popular. "Yes, I think it's required now; you have to do that [laughs]." (Jeff C.). "Yeah, we do that too. Pretty standard." (Thomas V.). "Oh yes, we go out to eat on Sunday. I don't have problem going out to eat." (Mike V.). "When I go to a restaurant my wife and I always pray before we eat; we pray out loud; we talk to the waitresses about church, their values and beliefs, etc. So when we do that on Sunday, we also try to witness to people about Sunday. Does God want restaurants open on Sunday? I don't know, my belief

---

[6]   Fred Meijer, *In His Own Words* (Grand Rapids, MI: Eerdmans, 1995), 152.

system, my Calvinistic belief system, I don't think so. One of the Ten Commandments is to keep the Sabbath holy. But today I do not have a problem; I don't play golf or go shopping or fill my car with gas on Sunday. But I will go out to eat to give my wife a break." (Albert I.). Sunday shopping creates uncomfortable feelings among several CEOs. "No—shopping—we definitely don't do it, unless it is a necessity." (Thomas V.). "I don't do that; I'm not going to say that I've never gone. But I don't make it a habit. I do go to the restaurant on Sunday now, for brunch." (James M.). "Yeah, I try not to. If I need to, I do. I think trying to keep some sanctity to Sunday and make it somewhat of a special day, we still try to." (Jeff C.). But the opposition against Sunday openings has gone: "Twenty-five years ago . . . It was a big thing when someone was open on Sunday or someone opened their store on Sunday or their restaurant. Over time that's gone away. Being closed on Sunday in this community now, there're not many people that really interpret that one way or the other. It's more generational, and as the generations that saw that as a significant issue get older, it just becomes less and less of an issue." (Luke Z.).

Did Dutch-American CEOs generally accept the rules prescribed by the Reformed or Christian church they grew up in, or was there a phase of rebellion? It appears that compliance was the dominant response, and rebellion was usually mild. "I don't recall any particular times of rebellion as such." (Harry V.). "I pretty much accepted the rules." (Mark F.). "I always felt it was the way it was supposed to be." (Victor H.). "Accepted it. My dad was very strict. Not loving. My mother was loving and strict as well. I rebelled one time: one night my buddies and I decided to take off and drive out to Florida. Could not find a job and returned. My parents never punished me and never talked about it afterwards." (Albert I). "A period of rebellion, yeah a little bit but not a lot." (Dale Z.). "I accepted early." (Robert H.). "I accepted the faith and the theology, not sure how much, it wasn't much of a driver for me on an everyday basis. I didn't rebel so much as I wanted my own way and did what I wanted to do." (Jerry V.). "Well I think I would say that I respected the rules." (Gene H.). "I bent the rules a little. It wasn't like I was doing anything bad, but with six kids you could sneak out and do whatever you want, and I kind of did." (Jeff C.). "I did to a degree. I got caught for shooting out street lights and was [put] on probation here [by a] judge; that gave my mother all kinds of heartburn." (Mike V.).

Fierce rebellion, we may conclude, was not an issue that characterized the formative years of our sample of highly successful entrepreneurs. This is particularly true for the older generation of

CEOs. Compliance with the rules was very much part of their Calvinist upbringing and its underlying theology of respecting authority. But there are also cases of more overt rebellion. "I wouldn't even begin to tell you about a lot of things I did. I did go into the alcohol thing, and partying, and all kinds of things my folks would not condone. That caused a lot of friction at home, for which I am sorry to this day." (Matt H.). But overall, rebellious behavior by Dutch-American entrepreneurs in their youth was the exception rather than the rule.

Having analyzed in quite some detail how CEOs look back at their upbringing is a good basis for exploring how the values and norms they were taught influenced their later career. This topic relates to the key question of this study. Do highly successful Dutch-American entrepreneurs believe that their upbringing provided a solid foundation—directly or indirectly—for their later success in business? And if so, which values and norms in particular are the ones that made the difference? Here is how CEOs responded to this vital issue: "The work ethic certainly came out of that commitment to stay with what you do, and keep on doing it. That sense of being disciplined about what you do and how you run your life. The value system that many of us grew up with in western Michigan was a conservative system that said, you don't spend what you make. You reinvest it, you save, you prepare for the bad times. Very Calvinistic theology. There is accountability to God and a belief that someday there is a God to say okay what did you do with what I entrusted [to you], or gave you the opportunity to grow with your talents and your resources? I think that is a tremendous, tremendous driver." (Jerry V.). "Absolutely, yes. I think the Reformed world view is extremely consistent with involvement in business. The Reformed view is to redeem all aspects of the world and all aspects are basically God's creation. We should be seeking to engage and redeem, exalt in life, all aspects recognizing that there were certain behaviors that we were not able to do. You cannot lie, you cannot steal, you cannot use power inappropriately, and you must exercise justice and responsibility in your business activities. I am pretty good at what I do in business, and it's where my gift and talent is, and I think the Reformed tradition allows you to express that talent and take it to the world." (Dale Z.). "Yes. The values that you pick up. The responsibilities that you pick up, but also the duties that you pick up, there are just activities you do. And of course discipline: work requires discipline." (Mark F.). "Definitely, the work ethic." (James M.). "Absolutely. I think that was 90 percent of the reason. Other than God's plan, God's purpose, I believe in all of that. But Dad taught us to work hard; he was almost like a dictator. He worked with you side by side and helped; he had ideas. Good Dutch thinking." (Albert I.). "Absolutely, it did. Oh, yes. You want to get ahead, you wanted to succeed in what you did, and work hard." (Thomas V.). "Yes, definitely. The whole idea of the sensing a purpose and life being greater than oneself. Seeing yourself as part of a larger universe, believing in a superior being or a force that you have some responsibility to beyond yourself, being driven by a sense of purpose—doing good. Earning your prosperity honestly by doing something of value for society, not just making a quick buck. That all comes from our Reformed world view." (Harry V.).

Again it is especially the religious and not the ethnic part in the value equation: "I don't know if I would call it my Dutch-American heritage, I would say my work ethic out of my family, from my parents, and my religious values very much impacted what I became. I could have been German, I could have been English, I happened to be Dutch." (Matt H.). Religion is the main driving force. "I, without a doubt, would not be what I am if I didn't understand the journey of faith and doctrine. This recession has hit hard, but my background taught me to be patient and wait for things to come. It helped me." (Robert H.). "Being honest is a big thing, and I think you learn that by being in church and knowing the Bible. And you don't lie, you are just honest with people." (John K.). "It is the best basis. The key concept of the Reformed background is that God is sovereign over every aspect of life. It is not just like God says, 'Go here.' God blesses me as I rely on him and as I go to him in my prayers. . . . I am in business because God guided me into this, and every day I am trying to figure out what God wants me to do with this business, because I have a beautiful business." (Mike V.).

It also affected the way business was done in the area. "Oh yes, because it gives your work ethic, and your ethic as far as a handshake or whatever, yep. The handshake business was a real niche in this area, based on trust, respect, and reputation. Your word was your honor. A lot of it is because of their conservative Dutch background and their Christian background." (Gene H.).

In conclusion: Dutch-American CEOs obviously link their entrepreneurial success to vital Reformed values and principles that in particular have to do with accountability, discipline, hard work, trust, honesty, and fairness. They feel that this value configuration was a solid foundation for a successful career as a business entrepreneur. These CEOs recognize that their entrepreneurial spirit—to paraphrase Max Weber—clearly benefited from the Calvinist ethos that dominated their upbringing. The worldview and behavioral repertoire that underlie their

Reformed education were a genuine force that clearly had an impact on their career. They believe that their worldly success is firmly rooted in their religious socialization. Their Reformed upbringing equipped them well with qualities needed for successful business careers.

CHAPTER 6

Norms, Values, and Entrepreneurial Success

The subjective assessment in the previous chapter of the basic relationship between Reformed upbringing and values needed for success in business calls for a further exploration of *how* Dutch-American CEOs relate their business success to entrepreneurial qualities. How do they define entrepreneurial success, what separates successful from non-successful entrepreneurs, and how have their Reformed values influenced some of their strategic business choices, their interaction with customers, and their employee policies? Do Reformed ethics matter? Do they themselves see that being raised in the Reformed tradition had an impact on other successful Dutch-American entrepreneurs as well? These are the main questions that I will explore in this chapter.

Features of Successful Entrepreneurs

The first topic in this context is how Dutch-American CEOs who evidently are highly successful themselves, characterize the personal qualities that make for a successful entrepreneur. How do these qualities relate to some of the traits we discussed in the first part of this study, such as dynamic leadership, innovation, creativity, seizing opportunity, pro-activeness, risk taking, and perseverance? And, of course, how do these entrepreneurs' traits connect to central Reformed values and norms? Analyzing the responses of CEOs shows a number of decisive characteristics associated with entrepreneurial success: creativity, vision, values, commitment, hard work, and determination. Creativity is a prime quality of a successful entrepreneur. "I think that the successful entrepreneur has an element of creativity about him. I don't know if it is innovation or research, but you have a creative bent to you." (Peter B.). "I think the key to most entrepreneurs is that they have an idea, and they want to put that idea into service. And the ones who do the best, are the ones who serve others the best. Now again there is a little bit of Dutch and a little bit of Reformed world view. Below that there are all kinds of things, there's creativity, there is discipline, and there is a measure of toughness that is absolutely critical. I think that the Reformed idea cultivates creativity and encourages creativity. God gave us the gift, the ability to create and to conceive ideas. And entrepreneurs can typically see unmet needs, see something that does not exist, see something and make it better." (Dale Z.). "If you are going to create a substantial organization, you have to create a culture where people share their creative energy in terms of helping to solve those problems as part of a team, [and] they have to be rewarded and encouraged for what they do. I think people [who] are long-term successful, especially multi-generationally successful, I think, figure out how to make that system work and create a culture that perpetuates that beyond themselves, whether you would attribute that to a particular religion or not. I think it helps to have a sense of purpose beyond yourself. A lot of great companies sort of have a religious culture or fervor in one way or another, some are literally religious, some not." (Harry V.). "Number one, the successful entrepreneur or person who builds the business is open to a variety of personalities and a variety of ideas. Think outside of the box. Number two, you have to be very comfortable with chaos. Many people like formality, process, routine, procedure. Personally, I'm very comfortable with chaos, keeping all kinds of different balls up in the air. At a certain point, you do need to develop process and routine and structure and discipline. But early on as you're birthing a company or an idea, to put some of those constraints on too early is very detrimental to the process. Number three, you cannot be afraid to fail, or you cannot be afraid of failure, because you will. And you cannot take that too personally; you need to learn from it. Number four, a great product or idea is only one slice of the pie. And you have all these other activities that need to come around it for it to be an ultimate success. Your idea needs to be engineered or marketed or distributed." (Luke Z.).

Vision is another quality of successful entrepreneurs that is mentioned by many CEOs. "You have to know where you are going; you need vision. I have [been] given the ability of vision, to see where I have to go. And you need structure to support your vision. Calvinist structure of faith." (Robert H.). A further necessary trait is the right combination of personality, common sense, and a commitment to people. "I think it's got an aspect of common sense, of personal responsibility, of creativity. There has to be some perseverance, and I think Calvinism gives you that. There's personal initiative. There also is some aspect where (there are probably entrepreneurs who pursued things individually) but it seems to go a whole lot easier if you bring people around you. I think the Dutch are good at that too. There's the social aspect of how the Dutch do things." (Adrian D.). "Well, if I were to write a business book, it'd be very brief and probably wouldn't sell very well. But there's a common sense for the uncommon person. So there's something that leads you to see what to you is just common sense. . . . When you talk to Meijer—well who wouldn't put grocery and general merchandise together? Who wants to make two stops? Nobody else did it before; well who wouldn't?" (Mark F.). "I think the number one is you have to get along with people. And you have to have the right people, good people with the same values and the same culture and who want to help [you] grow and become successful. The only way to do that is to work hard, to think, to be on the cutting edge." (Albert I.). "I think that I happen to have the kind of personality that I try to make friends with everyone, and I have got so many friends, and they have helped me through the years a lot of different ways, but I think friendship." (Victor H.).

Entrepreneurship is not just about creativity and vision, but also about the right values and about determination and hard work. "I think absolute honesty, transparent integrity is important for an entrepreneur. An entrepreneur is a leader, the team leader." (Mike Veldkamp). "It is all about honesty and integrity." (Gene H.). "Perseverance and pride. A higher level of commitment and hard work. Maybe confused priorities; maybe they should have spent more time with their family, but they were out working all the time." (David S.). "Sheer grit and determination; it was working sometimes right through the night on into the next day." (James M.). "There has to be some level of tenacity, dedication, determination and then there has to be a considerable amount of flexibility. . . . And trusting people outside of your own culture. Because you can be entrepreneurial to a degree, but if you keep it with the family or culture there are inherent limits as to how big it can get. Immigrants bring the tenacity and the entrepreneurial drive, but you've got to get beyond your own community to sustain it." (Rick P.). "I always look for three qualities in a successful person, and they are intelligence, hard work, and good ethics. And I believe those are three qualities that are very important for successful entrepreneurs." (Jerry V.). And there is no entrepreneurship without failure and mistakes. "An entrepreneur can't be afraid to make a mistake, because a mistake is a wonderful way of learning." (Mike V.).

A successful entrepreneur, so it can be concluded, has this unique combination of a smart idea and the ability to frame this idea within a larger creative vision, to seize the opportunity at the right time and pick the right people to build the business, to stick to his vision with the right mix of dedication and hard work, and to have the personal values and leadership qualities to sustain the vision and be seen as a role model in the business world and the community. Many of these qualities, as we saw, are related (directly or indirectly) to the values that are central to the Reformed tradition and the Reformed world view.

Risk-Taking

As outlined in Part I of this study, there is a long debate in the literature whether risk-taking is an intrinsic quality of successful entrepreneurship. Here is how greatly successful Dutch-American CEOs see the relationship between risk taking and success in business and how they link risk-taking to the worldview of Reformed thought. Dutch-American CEOs, not surprisingly, emphasize that willingness to take risks is an essential part of entrepreneurship. "I believe in order to be successful, we had to take risks. And the risks we took in this business were very, very important, and unless we have a risk-taking mentality, this company isn't getting any bigger." (Matt H.). "Without a doubt. And, it's a cliché, if you don't have a stomach or appetite for risk, innovating, building a new product or company, then you're not going to be very successful. If an entrepreneur won't take a calculated risk, then they can't be an entrepreneur. You're always working to reduce risk, but there's always going to be a certain amount of risk that's inherent in what you do, and you have to be comfortable with that." (Mike V.). "It's huge. My father before he died, one of the things he never thanked, [he was] never much on complimenting, but he did once say, 'I have to say to you, if I understood the risks that you undertook, we would never have been here.'" (Robert H.). "Absolutely crucial, crucial. One of the leaps we went into was credit on delivery. We didn't have enough money to give the credit to the customers." (Thomas B.). "Business has to have a certain dynamism. The entrepreneur as distinguished from other small business owners has that sense of possibility and that sense of growth. The small business owner may accept the status quo and either do very well or go out of business depending if I've got the right product and the right location. But in our case there was that big leap from the corner store which had existed for a couple of generations to the superstore. Kind of like the immigrants, only an entrepreneur was going to make that leap." (Rick P.). But it is calculated risk, not blind risk. "The goal in business is not to increase your risk; the goal in business is to reduce your risk. The person who is able to find a way to advance his position while taking the least risk possible—that is the prudent business man. The gamblers don't survive long term, and that is where a bit of culture comes in. Dutch culture which says be responsible, be thrifty." (Dale Z.). "Measured risk, sure. The adrenaline of the measured risk, the adrenaline of the deal; whatever you buy, somebody else didn't. Pretty simple. I think an entrepreneur needs that adrenaline rush of putting things together." (Mark F.). "I remember when I started up the business, I said what's the worst that can happen? It wasn't like we were destined or providential or anything like that, but looking at life that money was not the factor. I didn't get into it to make money. So the worst thing is, alright we've got a second mortgage on the house, and we would sell the house, and we would get an apartment. And we'd start over. Okay, it's not the end of the world. But I always felt from a faith standpoint, and maybe it was just a confidence and just an assuredness as to if it was meant to be then it was meant to be." (Jeff C.).

Various respondents linked risk-taking to their personal faith and the existential certainty it provides: God's care reduces worldly fears. God cares and gives you comfort. "You have to be risk-friendly. There's an aspect that goes with risk, of being not necessarily bold, but not fearing things. If you confront your fears and go boldly forward, it's amazing what you can accomplish. Our future rests in our Creator. So we have him to fear, no one else, and that's very appropriate. That's very comforting. I think the early colonists felt that same respect. It took a lot of initiative. Man! You had to really be bold. Leave your family behind. You had to be confident in the future." (Adrian D.). "Oh, no question about the need for risk-taking. That, to me, is just assumed. If statistically you hear that nine out of ten businesses fail, you either have to be a little bit naive or a little bit arrogant to even try it, right?

But I think the Reformed culture takes a little bit of risk out of the equation in your mind, because you think 'God's going to take care of me.'" (David S.). Dutch-American Reformed CEOs see risk-taking as an important dimension of entrepreneurship. It is in their minds an imperative condition for success. But they go one step further. Their Reformed faith puts secular fears in a somewhat different perspective: it diminishes the fear of failure as it provides confidence and comfort.

Values and Corporate Strategy

Next, these CEOs were asked to provide examples of how their personal values and norms as taught in their youth and embedded in the Reformed tradition influenced their entrepreneurial choices with respect to strategy, customers, and personnel. In some cases this impact is highly intentional and visible. Amway Corporation, for instance, explicitly states its founding values: "Partnership," "Integrity," "Personal Worth," "Achievement," "Personal Responsibility," and "Free Enterprise."[1] Bouma Corporation defines its guiding principle as "Honor God in Everything That We Do," "Do the Right Thing," "Over-serve," "Employee Focused," "Can Do," "Safety," "Performance Excellence," "Creativity," and "Teaming."[2] Request Foods, another highly successful company founded by a Dutch-American entrepreneur, is very explicit in its faith-based mission statement: "To honor God in all we do, to help people develop, to pursue excellence, and to grow profitable."[3] Their first two core values (honor God and commitment to excel) clearly link faith and work ethic. Honor God: "God provides the ultimate standard for our conduct. With the goal of honoring God in our decisions and actions, we will choose to be honest, fair, courteous, and professional. We are dedicated to placing priority on Christian principles in every aspect of our business." Commitment to Excel: "With a proactive work ethic, we choose to freely give and be receptive to new and constructive ideas. We accept responsibility to mentor one another, as well as to overcome obstacles. Our relentless goal is to do it right the first time."[4] Mission statements are important as basic representations of the enterprise's purpose for existence and to highlight socially meaningful values the

---

1   Their vision statements highlight: "Helping People Live Better Lives," "Helping Consumers Live Better Lives," "Helping IBOs Live Better Lives," "Helping Employees Live Better Lives," and "Helping Neighbors Live Better lives" (see http://www.amway.com/en/about-amway/vision-values).
2   See: http://www.boumacorp.com/boumacorpculture.html.
3   See: http://www.requestfoods.com/.
4   See: http://www.requestfoods.com/copacker.html.

enterprise seeks to realize. But their factual significance is in how this vision translates into observable actions, that is, in terms of strategic choices, how the company wants to come across to customers, or how it treats its employees. How do business ethics enter corporate decision making and what is the relationship with Reformed moral principles?

Let us first have a look at strategic corporate choices and decisions. Is there a role of values, of faith? Particularly in hard economic times, and at the level of the entrepreneur as an individual, the answer is affirmative. "As CEO I had to make some very challenging business decisions, to restructure the company, to transition the business from the first generation of leadership to a subsequent generation of leadership, be it family or non-family leadership, but to be that bridge from a very powerful first generation. Or, as I say, to build a bridge from a culture of personality to a culture of ideas. I had to make choices and decisions that did not make me very popular at my family's Thanksgiving table. But in retrospect, they all, thankfully, to their credit, have all said yeah, you were right. I had to make some tough decisions, push hard on some things, within the family, that they did not want to hear or want to do. My faith helped me greatly. If your faith does not affect your management style, you'd better think real hard about what you say your faith view is." (Dale Z.). "I did a major expansion in the late 1980s, and that was the only time I put myself on the line after I began in 1980. And later the GM [General Motors] bankruptcy, that really hit me. The market was down 60 percent. It was out of my hands. That was a time in my life, in my business life, that I've really felt dependent on God." (Mark F.). "I've had my share of failures. There was this major business deal I was involved in. I had put together a $100 million financing package. Then a major funder withdrew. We had paid for the entire deal. The transaction was complete except for the check three days before they were supposed to fund. Some of my sub-contractors already started the work. If I failed, I'd sink their companies too. I really was in trouble. There was fear. I could lose the whole thing. My faith really helped me. The understanding that life is temporal, that we're in God's hands. Fortunately, a group of people [well-known Dutch-American entrepreneurs] came alongside me and created a temporary bridge that helped me out." (Adrian D.). "When I wake up, I pray. I just pray for wisdom and direction. Twenty years ago I asked, 'God where do you want to take this $20 million company?' We'll do $250 million in sales this year, so I ask 'God, where do you want to take us next year?' I pray for God's direction, for God's leading. If you don't have a vision, you're going to perish. That's Biblical." (Albert I.). "Well, I think I would go back and look at my career and I would just say that the more difficult times were when you really felt like the lone ranger, yes some significant decisions to make, and you just finally have to make it. You can gather all kinds of data, information, you finally have to make that decision. You know God is going to be available for you to share with. And what we are doing is, this stuff isn't ours, you know, we have been very, very fortunate, but we have an accountability here that, whether it's time or talent or resources or finances. Where would you be without faith?" (Peter B.). "When I went through economic hard times, I literally went through understanding this is a gift from God, if it has to close, or has to open, it has to continue; it's beyond my ability to manage this, that's how I got through that." (Robert H.). "I was this close a couple times to losing the business. I can remember lying awake, practically on the Monday of the week I had no idea how I was going to make payroll on Friday. That was several times. Having to make a decision to go in debt. . . . I hated going in debt, you know, and having to borrow money to buy that next piece of equipment or to do something or to get our own building. My faith definitely helped. I think it definitely did. I think from a standpoint of God's sovereignty and it's much bigger than just this, right? As difficult as this is, it's peanuts compared to everything else." (Jeff C.).

Not all of the CEOs see a direct relationship between vision, strategy, and values. Some perceive a more indirect link. "We have always been in a fairly disciplined strategic planning process that I would not say is the values base, it is probably more to do with ability to attract and retain talent that shares those values and ultimately having a vision for what you want to do with the business and why you want to do it. That certainly has something to do with values. Ultimately the strategies you do in terms of executing and adapting to the changing world—that is more business- than values-based." (Harry V.). "Usually the economic reality and finances will drive particular decisions. Now it could be the decision to pull the plug on something or to invest more and go deeper into something. But the human aspect really has a major influence. The economics and the financial picture may tell you this isn't going to happen. But you happened to have partnered with an entrepreneur or someone . . . you just like . . . as a person. They're passionate about their idea; you're passionate about the idea; you love the idea. That's where you do lie awake." (Luke Z.). "I would say that my ethics were a foundation; it was just there. Ethics didn't have anything to do with strategic decisions, we just felt it was an opportunity and a drive, our strategic directions have been influenced by what we perceived our assets and strengths to be." (Jerry V.).

The results, in short, show that faith, vision, and strategy are to some degree interrelated. But the strongest impact of faith, of the Reformed world view and thought, is evident when times are bad, when tough decisions have to be made, and when the company's future is at stake. That is where faith comes in, both as a source of comfort and as a source of bringing a larger perspective: the transcendence of the painful here and now.

Values and Customer Orientation

The next cluster of issues is related to the way in which faith, values, and upbringing affect enterprise-client relationships. Do they make a difference? Do they influence how successful Dutch-American entrepreneurs want their company to come across to their customers? Results demonstrate that in some cases the company's identification with Christianity is quite explicit and strong. "Most of our customers certainly know that we have Christian values, and we have a Christian base, and that we as individuals are Christians—because we don't hide it, and we're pretty open about it." (Chris G.). "Absolutely. Well, it's the extension of me; it's all they know about me. My name is on the building. And my faith and integrity are there every day; that's their only experience with me." (Mark F.). "We're not afraid to talk about our values. We don't work Sundays here. And we tell our customers that in twenty years we've never worked a Sunday. We've never shorted an order, because we'll work; however, we have to work six days a week to produce the products to fill the orders for our customers. And God has just provided that we could do it in six days. I think God has blessed us because we're honoring God and our customers." (Albert I.).

In many cases the CEOs' Reformed faith and company's roots translate primarily into fair treatment of customers. "Yes, absolutely. I was obligated as a matter of responsibility to care for my customers and not take advantage of them. Was it important that they identify me as a Christian? No, it was important that I conducted my affairs and the affairs of the business in a way that was consistent with my faith, and if they connected the two, it was fine. But I never wore my policy on my sleeve and said you should buy from me because I am a Christian, or to put stamps of fish on every product we send out the door." (Dale Z.). "Customers knew we were honest as the day is long, we were not going to take advantage of them, they knew we prayed before we ate." (Peter B.). "Yeah. You do what's right; you do what's fair. Customers know and understand that, and that's where the difference many times comes in. So, you're open and honest about your own mistakes and your own failings and your own shortcomings as a company. . . . It could be at your own detriment, but I think, again, if you have a long-term view, that customer is not just an order today, it's a long-term relationship. You have those shared values . . . but it isn't like you sit down and talk about all that, it is just there." (Jeff C.).

The CEO's ethnic roots may also play a role, for example, with respect to the proverbial Dutch punctuality and cleanliness. "We are 99 percent on time, our people wear uniforms, our facilities are as clean as possible, the floors are waxed, if you are going into our bathrooms, you could sleep there . . . really the structure we were brought up on is the foundation. But we don't over push the doctrine." (Robert H.). In various cases, finally, CEOs state that their religious values play a much more implicit role in customer relations, and that fair treatment, correctness, and trust are the chief values that matter. "I know our customers see the difference in the way we treat them, versus others. I don't think any of them would attribute it to Calvinism. I have some other partners who are deeply religious and some people might see the religious values expressed within the company, but we don't really preach the religion within the business, some businesses do, but we don't." (Harry V.). "I think that wherever we went, they could see the difference. You know, we didn't swear, we didn't swear at the people, but I didn't hold my religion at the end of my fingers. We tried, and yeah that's what made us successful—that and hard work." (John K.). "Not really, other than there are certain characteristics within us that make our partners comfortable working with us or our customers working with us. Do we do business with people because we are Reformed? Probably not much of that. Ten or fifteen years ago, you would hear companies characterize themselves as a Christian company, now you really don't hear that anymore, but what you will hear is that, 'that CEO goes to my church,' or 'He's a Christian,' or 'That company is led by a great group of people.'" (Luke Z.). "It can become self-serving to talk about these things. I don't think it's important to convey some kind of religious or political value. Because the business we're in, there's a value of trust that it's very much in our self interest to convey, but very important to convey, because people are relying on us and that's a much more fundamental trust than an occasional purchase of some other commodity." (Rick Post).

On balance, it can be concluded that companies differ in the way their Reformed or Christian roots and values are conveyed to their customers. In some cases this is very direct and explicit; in other cases it is more indirect and implicit. The position of the company on this dichotomy is very much determined by the degree of outspokenness of the company's CEO on this topic. In all cases, however, CEOs underline the importance of fairness and honesty as values governing customer relations.

Values and Personnel Policy

The third and final issue under this theme of the impact of a CEO's personal religious values on entrepreneurial decisions—after strategic visions and customer relations—is the way that these values affect the company's personnel policies. Is there a direct link between the two sets of values? or is the relationship more implicit and more subtle? Does faith make a difference in the domain of personnel policy? "Yes, absolutely, because my faith wouldn't allow me to abuse my employees. I was obligated as a matter of responsibility to care for my people and not take advantage of them. As a Christian I believe that all of human kind are uniquely created individuals. Therefore no matter what my job is, I stand shoulder to shoulder with every other person who works in this organization, because while their design may be different than mine, we all have the same master architect." (Dale Z.). "We are doing well because we've hired good people. We've taken care of our people. They all get a pay increase every year. We have a performance-based objective plan. If the company makes more money, they get bonuses and bigger bonuses. And every year we've been able to give all of our people bigger bonuses, from the lowest person to the highest person. They've got to do their job. People on the line have to come to work every day and do the best job they can; they've got to come to work on time, and we will reward them. If the company does a good job, they get rewarded." (Albert I.). "Very definitely, I would say that was very, very definitely a big part of that. We tithed the company money. We had a Share & Care program where the company would match donations by our employees. We've given millions away." (James M.). "It does. We have a very liberal tuition reimbursement program to fund people that want to go to school, part time or Saturdays. We have done that for years and years. A lot of people have expanded their education this way." (Matt H.). "I always felt a strong employee responsibility. Growing up, I always remember the conversation around the dinner table. As for what can we do, whether it was instituting a Christmas party for the company or giving hams at Christmas or instituting a new bonus program, or when we had particularly successful year, announcing a companywide significant hourly wage increase, and that came from Dad's ethics that this is what you did. He cared about his employees and has also been an influence throughout my life. We pay a fair wage, our benefit package is pretty good." (Jeff C.). Treating your people well may increase their empowerment. "Within this organization we always felt that, as an employee, I'm an owner in the organization; I'm responsible for the organization's success. There was very little top down, mandated activity. You were empowered; you were given a lot of independence." (Luke Z.). Some CEOs explicitly address the issue of a multi-religion employee force. "We had a lot of people working for us, Christians and non-Christians. There would be the quarterly meeting, and I would get up and pray, for the company but also for their families." (Peter B.). One CEO is more outspoken on this issue. "We have a lot of Hispanics and Asians working for us. We don't try to . . . we want people to become Christian and know the Lord Jesus Christ, our Savior, but we don't preach it; we show it; we walk it; we talk it a little bit. And we're winning, we're winning." (Albert I.). "Our mission statement of our company, which hung on the wall of every office said our number one [purpose] was to serve God. And we were going to do that by donating a percentage of our profits to worthy Christian charities, and by dealing with people fairly and with integrity. I had people who were agnostics or atheists working for me who said, 'One of the reasons I worked here . . . I liked this company because of the mission statement.' 'Well, do you believe it?' 'No, but I think it's a good set of rules.'" (David S.).

Various CEOs emphasize the importance of role modeling. "You teach by example rather than trying to create an enclave of Christians." (Adrian D.). "We don't create doctrine here, we don't spell [out our] beliefs, but from our values and what I believe this company is here for, as long as we are serving, we are serving our employees, we are serving the people who work here, and they are serving back." (Robert H.). "They know how we feel, all the employees that are close to us. They know what, how we feel about them, like last Sunday, my wife and I had to go to a funeral home, and the man that worked for me forty-some years, had muscular dystrophy, his mother-in-law passed away, so we went to see him, I talked to him. I helped him. They all know that we try to do our best." (Gene H.). The rule of treating your employees fairly and honestly is highlighted by all CEOs.

Fair employee treatment, finally, can be pretty far-reaching, as illustrated by the following CEO statement: "An entrepreneur can't be afraid to make a mistake, because a mistake is a wonderful way of learning, everyone I work with knows that I don't jump on them. I lost two-thirds of a million dollars this week, and I am still dying about that, because a mistake was made here in one of our departments, and I am not [saying] that I don't get it, you can tell that my blood boiled, just raised a little bit. But I said to them, alright, that is a mistake, alright don't make it again, and it was two-thirds of a million dollars that went out the window." (Mike V.).

As was the case with respect to customer relations, the individual CEO is very deliberate in the domain of personnel policy also. If there is a direct and explicit relationship between religious values, customer relations, and employee policies, this is often because the individual CEO is very outspoken on these issues. Vice versa, if this impact is more indirect and implicit, it is because the individual CEO has a more subtle point of view on these topics. Not because he or she is less religious, but because the CEO applies a more multi-faceted approach.

It is important to emphasize in this context that in all cases we are dealing with self-reports which may reflect a certain positivity bias and may be subject to social desirability. Respondents after all were not provided a strong incentive to give a balanced account of all the positive and negative impact of their company's customer and personnel policies. And these policies were not checked by me. On the other hand, we are dealing with strong personalities that are not particularly in need to comply with socially desirable answers vis-à-vis their impact in these domains. Again, this study is not on objective accuracy but on subjective significance.

The final question to be answered here is whether our CEOs see the assumed impact of being raised in a Dutch-American culture and in the Reformed faith on other successful Dutch-American entrepreneurs as well. Do they see striking parallels? Do they believe that success in business is somehow related to Dutch-American upbringing and Reformed values? Do successful Dutch-American CEOs have certain characteristics in common? Here is how they responded: "Well, I will certainly link faith and entrepreneurship. Dutch-American, I can link into it. I don't mean to be biased here ethnically, but I see for instance an Italian entrepreneur—Christian or not—has a different approach to life." (Mike V.). "People in West Michigan, especially the Dutch people, are out of a risk-taking culture—their ancestors decided to pull up stakes in their country and leave it for one reason or another. Now that isn't an easy thing to do. Very risky, those people had risk in their genes to begin with, and those genes were passed onto some of us luckier people in West Michigan, and so I think that risk taking is a very integral part of our culture. It still is today, and there are all kinds of businesses around here. You think, how in the heck did that start? It started because someone laid awake at night and thought, I want to take risks; I am willing to risk my career and go for it." (Matt H.). "I would say the majority of them are probably pretty strong Christians, and you hear and you learn that God gives you gifts to use. I don't know whether other nationalities approach it from that way. I mean, like the talents, if you hide your talent, those are sins of omission of what you don't do with what you've been given. And also I think just to be able to share the joy of doing a job and doing it well and the joy of being able to give and to help and so on. And that comes from a spiritual background." (James M.). "I think there is velocity to energy, from the heritage, that, there are a lot of people who said, 'I can't find a solution for that.' That is not our background. Our background says there must be a solution; let's work hard to find one. If you look at our area, it's interesting how many of the successful businesses actually come from that heritage." (Peter B.). "I find that the Dutch have a unique gift: they are loyal and they are determined." (Robert H.). "You know, the Dutchmen are good for starting a company and they take their sons in. It's all family." (Victor H.).

There is indeed a regional linkage. One CEO points at the winning combination of culture and character that makes West Michigan a fertile area for successful entrepreneurship. "It has more to do with personality and some of our own character traits. Now what I think does happen in West Michigan and why a lot of companies in the area have been successful is that if you bring some of the Dutch-Reformed foundational characteristics alongside the characteristics of successful entrepreneurs; that's an incredible combination." (Luke Z.). Others, finally, see the unique convergence of employer-employee value and more general Calvinist values as a major asset of the area. "I believe that many of the original entrepreneurs were successful because their employees had the same values. The entrepreneurs can't take all the credit, much of the credit needs to go to the organization, because those are the people that every day and in every way, through their faiths, did the right thing for the right reasons. I no longer consider us a Dutch Calvinist society in western Michigan; we now have a significant number of employees from Hispanic and Asian heritage. I think immigration is the salt in any society, and you get the brightest and the best when you invite immigrants in. We still have the same quality work ethic, but I can no longer describe it as Dutch Calvinist." (Jerry V.). "I'm not so sure that the Reformed or CRC is as big of a driver as it is just the general Calvinist values, and I'm not sure that it's really Reformed that drives that as much as it is kind of the general Protestant/Calvinistic values which you can find in a lot of different places." (Chris G.).

The picture that emerges from these statements is that highly successful Dutch-American entrepreneurs in West Michigan share a can-do mentality, are willing to take risks, are solution-oriented, take responsibility, and have people working for them with the right work ethos. This combination of features is strongly believed to be determined by basic Calvinist values. The ethnic component in this picture is somewhat diffuse and is particularly underlined by the older generation of entrepreneurs. The culture of Calvinism, character and commitment in West Michigan is, according to our sample of highly-successful CEOs, a solid and fertile breeding ground for excellent entrepreneurship.

Lifestyle, Charity, and Politics

Personal Lifestyle

The CEOs in this study are all wealthy people; millionaires and even some billionaires. Their success as entrepreneurs has brought them great affluence. This raises the question of how our sample of Reformed and Christian Reformed entrepreneurs sees the relationship between Biblical, and more specifically Calvinist, teachings and personal lifestyle. In Max Weber's thesis on the Protestant ethic and the spirit of capitalism, the asceticism of the Calvinist entrepreneurs in the seventeenth and eighteenth centuries stressed a frugal and plain lifestyle that refrained from hedonism and conspicuous consumption.[1] Profits from one's entrepreneurial activities were supposed to be reinvested in the company and not to be used for personal pleasure-seeking. Entrepreneurial success was seen as a blessing, as a sign of virtue, and of God's election. Greed, materialism, and self-indulgence

---

[1] Renowned German Protestant Theologian Ernst Troeltsch spoke of "Reformed Asceticism," *Die Bedeutung des Protestantism für die Entstehung der modernen Welt* (Tübingen: Mohr, 1924), 43.

were believed to be inconsistent with the puritan Protestant ethic. How do contemporary entrepreneurs with strong roots in the Calvinist tradition interpret the lifestyle consequences of Biblical teachings? Is personal wealth indeed a blessing from God, a token of his grace? What is, from their perspective, the relationship between faith and fortune? It is a complex and also sensitive issue.

"Is it okay for Christians to be rich? If I had a concern, that would be it. We are taking too much for granted. Blessings we get are from the Lord all the time. Wealth is a sign of God's grace. Completely. I have no trouble with that at all. The moment you deny that, you're also denying God." (Victor H.). For some entrepreneurs the differential impact of blessing and grace is hard to understand. "Why has my family been blessed? The truth is I don't know. I honestly don't know. My father did very well, but how do I account for the difference that someone who also worked very hard, did not. I don't know how to. So I simply say, okay, it's by God's grace." (Dale Z.). "Oh, absolutely. I didn't earn anything; I really didn't. I didn't earn it. You look at the timing of why certain things happen. I don't think I was any smarter or anything else. You say yeah, the hard work, the risk-taking, all those things, but there're lots of people out there that'll work just as hard, or smarter than I am or risk-taking, and they haven't been blessed the way we have. So, yeah, being blessed beyond certainly what you think you deserved is definitely part of our thinking." (Jerry V.). "Yes, clearly. I'm not as smart as [would seem to be the case because] I earned money. There're a lot of guys who work eighteen hours a day [but] don't have any money. So it isn't just hard work; it isn't brilliance." (David S.).

What is clear, is that, according to CEOs, wealth creates responsibility. "Without a doubt, but it's a huge responsibility. I feel it's God's money that he has entrusted to me." (James M.). "Absolutely, it is. sometimes you don't always understand why He does things; it comes from His divine hand, not from me. I guess that's part of my upbringing, but that's what I believe in." (Chris G.). "It's a blessing but no greater blessing than sitting with your family at Ottawa Beach yesterday on an eighty-three-degrees sunny day. It's also a burden. The responsible management of it is huge." (Mark F.). "Absolutely, but I also believe God is blessing us because we're trying to make a difference in our people's lives here. We don't work Sundays; we don't overwork our people; we don't take from them financially. And if the profits are better here, I don't take it all; I could. But it's a choice we make to spread it among all of our people here." (Albert I.). "Wealth comes with responsibility. I would characterize it as a level of responsibility. I think that that's directly related to the Reformed world view. My parents taught us that not giving was not an option. Non-negotiable. They started that early in their relationship. They would tell us stories that when they first got married my mother would take 10 percent and put it in the envelope to give it away." (Dale Z.). "It's still all God's and you cannot get carried away [as though it were] yours. We are having a little of a struggle with that, because we are building a house, because you kind of stop, there is no mortgage or anything like that, okay well are we doing enough in the kingdom? This isn't ours; you don't tack a bank bag on to the back of the hearse or anything like that. But I believe it was just God's lead allowing us to be successful, allowing us to create the value that we created." (Peter B.).

Affluence is a blessing but may lose its meaning across generations. "Oh yes, we call it a blessing. But when you start looking at the kids, and the grandkids, then you see, wealth isn't always the best. The kids all got money, you know. They take it for granted." (Thomas V.).

Do CEOs enjoy the fruit of their hard work? Do they take pleasure in luxury? Do worldly goods give them satisfaction? "If a frugal lifestyle is living within your means, then I suggest that anybody you're interviewing is living well within their means while still being generous with their funds. It's all relative to what you have."(Mark F.). "When you become wealthy—and I'm the president of a [multi-] million [dollar] company—I could treat my people like, 'I'm this man!' But I don't; but it takes some work to do that. I drive a Lexus, been driving a Lexus for fifteen years; it's the best quality car made, I believe. But I don't care if my people see that. I dress common. Well, anyway I just want to be like common folks. We have a beautiful home on Lake Macatawa. I've got a little boat—a twenty-six-footer; I used to have a fifty-footer. We take people on the boat—you be yourself. Don't be somebody that you're not." (Albert I.). "I can share with you that having grown up here and having lived in Los Angeles, I have a perception of Los Angeles that many, many people lived beyond their means. They tried to live a glitzier, fancier lifestyle than they really could afford. When I came here and reflected back on that, I knew many families who lived dramatically below their means, and I thought living in that showy way was improper, and that would have certainly come out of Calvinism, clearly that Calvinist mindset. Not that you shouldn't prosper, but stay humble, and live your life to the glory of God, not to [your own] glory." (Harry V.). "Basically I don't need much. My wife doesn't need much. When you are wealthy, you have two choices: one is leaving your money to the family to maneuver or grow, or another one is to spend some of it now on charity and good causes. And I'm spending it. I'm spending quite a lot." (Thomas B.). "It does all boil down to Genesis 12:2[2] and whether you're affluent, like some of us that you happen to be interviewing, or at a different level of affluence, I think that all of us need to understand that we weren't given these blessings so we can buy bigger and bigger toys. There are a few people around here that do that, and they have in my estimation at least, a lot more toys than they really need, but that is not really for me to decide, they also do a heck of a lot, and it's relative to where you are on the scale." (Matt H.). "Wealth is a gift from God. Whatever I have is not mine. It's just like when we built this house twelve years ago, people say, 'Man what a nice house,' and it is a beautiful house, and we have a beautiful setting and everything. But I said you ought to see what my heavenly home is going to look like; that means a lot more than the house or whatever it is. Because in our life, you know, people that are from the world you might say, they look at all the frills, you know." (Gene H.).

Finding the right balance between blessings and the human factor is not an easy challenge. "In our tradition here, it's really not part of our being to show our wealth or to be showy. It's part of our personality in the Reformed tradition to play down those things. At times it's a struggle to be blessed with success and resources and wealth and try to reconcile that with the Reformed tradition. It's a real challenge. You hear, 'It's not ours, everything belongs to God.' That's a little cliché, and sometimes I think that that comes out of people's mouths a little quickly. We're all human and flawed, and it doesn't take too long to start considering God's money as your money when you're writing checks and doing deals and being successful. We sold this company for five times what we have in it, didn't we do great? It's just human nature to think that way. We are constantly wrestling with reconciling being so blessed with what our responsibilities are." (Luke Z.).

It is clear from these findings that CEOs define their wealth and affluence in terms of God's blessings and grace. And this is, of course, the correct Calvinist interpretation. Reformed doctrine teaches that personal prosperity is not merely and only a direct effect of personal skills, hard work, and fortunate risk-taking but has to do also with God's grace and larger plan. CEOs almost collectively embrace this interpretation. The doctrine explains but also legitimizes their prosperity. Simple observations show that our sample of highly successful and well-to-do Reformed entrepreneurs lead different

---

[2]   "I will make of you a great nation, and I will bless you, and make your name great, so that you will be a blessing," (NRSV).

lifestyles, that is, from a materialist point of view. Some show their wealth and property, whereas others opt for a more modest way of living. But without exception, they all emphasize the responsibility that wealth creates: sharing and giving. This brings us to the topic of charity, a phenomenon that is huge in this part of the country.

Charity and Community Philanthropy

As outlined in the introduction: West Michigan has a culture of giving, a culture that is deeply rooted in the Reformed tradition of tithing. Traveling in this part of the country shows how charity has enabled an impressive number of substantial private initiatives in the domains of care, culture, education, and nature conservation. Sizable donations were made by my respondents. Grand Rapids and Holland, Michigan are visible and vivid examples of the generosity of successful Dutch-American entrepreneurs. The golden rule is that giving is expected from successful businessmen. Not giving is not an option. "Not giving is frowned upon. I know some people, typically first generation, who have been very successful, sold their business, and spent it on themselves and having fun, but do very little to give back to the community." (Harry V.). Giving has to do with wanting to make a difference in one's life, a difference outside the world of business success. "One thing I do is medical care, hospitals. When you get stories of things they're doing, it makes you feel kind of good. So I've reached the stage of life where I say it isn't the advertising; it's what we want to accomplish in our lifetime. Now I have two choices: one to grow the company bigger or to give it away. I think the company is a good enough base, it can go on from here, so I'll give away some money." (Thomas B).

As indicated earlier, personal wealth according to the CEOs comes with personal responsibility. Not as a burden but as an obligation to share. "I wouldn't characterize wealth as a burden. I would characterize it as a level of responsibility that others who have never been in the situation don't realize. They don't see it. Sometimes I express that my life is a little like a balance . . . with half the scale behind the curtain. The part that everyone sees is the blessing part, but there's a responsibility part that is behind the curtain, that giving wisely is the responsibility part." (Dale Z.). Wealth obliges; wealth means the calling to give. "My faith has taught me that a tithe or 10 percent of my income is expected of the least of us, and so that has caused my wife and me to ask the question [that] if this is expected of the least of us, what is expected of us, with the resources that we have? That has led us to strive to take that to 50 percent of our income, occasionally over that, sometimes below that." (Jerry V.). "With success comes a lot of responsibility. Something that's always been very important to our family and that my parents really engrained into us is giving back and that with success does come a lot of responsibility. And that was way before we had anything. Until the company sold, Dad just happened to have a good job. But there wasn't this over the top type of wealth and success. Since that time, being involved in a lot of different non-profits and charity organizations and giving back the financial resources has been a very important part of who we are. We really believe that because we have been blessed, we have to work really hard at making sure we're doing as much with that as possible. That includes giving back and continuing to be successful." (Luke Z.). "You thought it was important to not only run your company but also to help other people. I had a lot charity. I did a lot of that, so that I could feel that I was helping others too. Yeah I have more mail here than anyone else, but that's because I send out more checks than anyone else." (Victor H.). "There is no joy in having money. There's only joy in giving money. If you've got a pile of money under the bed, it's not really that much fun." (David S.). "I guess we do because we understand you can't take it with you, but I would always say, you can send it ahead, that's what I say, you can send it ahead." (John K.). "Like many of my friends who've made a lot of money at a young age, all I'm working for now is to give it away; that's really the main purpose, right?" (Mark F.). "Entrepreneurs here may be very wealthy but don't necessarily live that way. They plow their resources back into their company and help people grow, and they do things at times to help employees that are not a part of the formal benefit structure and stuff like that; philanthropy is exceptionally high. It is the second most philanthropic area in the United States." (Harry V.).

CEOs underline that giving and sharing is Biblical and embodied in the notion of stewardship. "I have done hundreds of millions [of dollars in] deals, and I have seen God in that, and I believe from the Scripture that I am just a steward of all these things. When I leave this earth, I won't take anything with me. I believe from Scripture that I am not called to leave everything to my kids and my grandkids where they are fabulously wealthy and can live off of a trust and so forth. I believe that I am called to use it wisely. So what does that mean? I think the bottom line for me is that I am using, I am trying to use God's money to his honor and to further his Kingdom. Now 'Kingdom' is a great Reformed word, and that is what I am trying to do, and whether I am trying to do it secretively through a business or underwriting this or . . . the next thing, I always try to do it to further God's Kingdom." (Mike V.). "We are taught to be stewards of all our resources, not only our monetary ones, our time resources, our talent resources; all those things we have been blessed with and how are we sharing those with the community. And that doesn't apply just to entrepreneurs. There is a tremendous community spirit of voluntarism in this community. This is an area that I experience stewardship, sacrificial stewardship." (Jerry V.).

My sample of highly successful CEOs receives numerous requests for donations and contributions from all sectors of society: church organizations, hospitals, schools, political parties and candidates, community organizations, interest groups, and many charitable organizations. Most of them have their own foundations to handle these requests professionally and to structure their charitable donations. How do CEOs decide where to put their money? Do they have a particular philosophy underlying their involvement in charity? And if so, how does this relate to their personal values and beliefs? The first principle is serving God and his plan for the world. "The main criterion is: is it going to further God's Kingdom?" (Mike V.). The church and the community are the main recipients. "The belief is helping the community out. If God blesses you, we've got to help the community. We give back a lot now. We more than tithe from our pretax profits. We like to keep the churches strong because without a church, this country is going to go down the tubes. Without the local church, what's going to happen? So we really support local churches and also Christian colleges. Salvation Army, we give to the Cancer Society some of those things, but not as much as the Christian, because secular companies give to them. We are very selective." (Albert I.). For some CEOs charity has become a professional business. "My wife and I have a process now, every quarter we review a list of requests, and so we sit down and now involve our children in that decision. And before we do it, my typical prayer before we start is, 'Lord give us open hearts and wise minds, so that we can discern what it is that we should [do], that there is a message that we are being led to that our heart should be softened to that, yet we should be wise and thoughtful and conscientious in our execution.' And so it's a business—to give money away wisely." (Dale Z.). At issue is whether to give anonymously or donate publicly for instance through fundraising parties. "Some believe that giving is to be done anonymously, so they may be very generous, but others don't know about it. I would say when I was a child, everyone had the ethic you gave anonymously. That was part of the Christian ethic. Other people do it more visibly like the DeVoses do, but that's a relatively new thing. They think carefully about what is important to the community; they would invite their friends around, and tell them we think this is important, we will do a disproportionate share and we want you to join us in doing this—kind of a group hug—so they do things visibly as a reminder of their prosperity and presentations that you are going to give back, we are doing it and we expect you to do it too. They have been doing absolutely great things." (Harry V.). "There is one building we donated that has our name on it. The first and probably last one. It gets back to our Reformed roots: don't brag about what you you've got. Be humble." (Luke Z.).

Another matter is whether CEOs donate to many different causes or focus on a more limited set of projects but with larger contributions. Donation strategies differ. "I look at what we donate and what we invest in; we make lots of little donations. I don't expect a lot; I don't expect people to keep me informed of what they are doing. But we have picked four endeavors that we invest in, and those things, those companies, those charities, we add several zeros to what we give to those people, and we expect a return. When we invest in the Boys and Girls Club, I expect to see some results in that. When we invest in international water missions and pay for water systems around the world, I want to see that they are working, what that money is doing. The same holds for our donations to the Church World Service of the RCA and our support for the college." (Matt H.). "I tend to put requests into three categories—you prioritize your passions, we did that with our children as they went through schools. Is it domestic? International? Missions? Gospel? Food? Education? Where is it? So then you prioritize into three categories [levels of interest or involvement]: (1) you're going to learn about, understand and perhaps engage in. And you tend to talk to the CEOs, and they'll call you. At that level that's who you want to hear from and learn exactly what's going on; (2) You might read the report; and (3) you just send them something because they're good. If you look on the left hand side of the letterhead, you tend to know most of the people." (Mark F.). This last remark is shared by other CEOs as well: if there is a name on the fund raisers list you know well, "it must be good." "Sometimes by the person who asks, but also we try to help for us. It's a goal to give mostly to Christian organizations: medical care and Christian schools. We give to some community, some public area to enhance the community, but mostly we concentrate on the Christian part of it. We have become more focused." (Gene H.). "In general our focus is on children. We just feel it's important for us to try to help kids that have the least ability to help themselves. But we're very careful with how we help kids and where we do; we don't just want to give somebody something. We want to make sure that when we help somebody, they're helping themselves or learning to help themselves—to empower them." (Chris G.). And for all CEOs, passion is important. "I serve because I have a reason. I can't serve without a reason; I am just not that kind of a guy; I have to serve for a reason and a passion."(Robert H.).

What are the main causes to which CEOs donate? The list is certainly impressive and the church, schools, and hospitals rank highly. "You get requests all over. I have people, but I do a lot of it myself. There are a lot of philanthropists that will give to arts and medicine and things like that. I feel it's God's money that he has entrusted to me and my heart is for the people who are lost. So that is why I give to Christian schools, church organizations, ministries that are out there making a difference in young people's lives—or a para-church organization that's Christ-like. That's why I've got to be busy, because I've got to be sure they're using this money for something that's building young people up." (James M.). "Mostly local things. Like the new hospital. Our church. And we support the college." (Thomas V.). "You get a lot of letters. My wife and I have a certain list; you get on that list, you get money every year. Got to have some connection to the Christian. And you kind of follow what these groups are doing. We gave a lot of money to our church and to the college." (John K.). "I think everybody has their own types of things. Ours is Christian education and next the church."(Jerry V.). "We receive hundreds and hundreds of requests and there're some characteristics that we're always looking for. We support our churches, educational institutions that we are associated with, Christian schools, the college. We have a really soft spot for the impaired, disabled, mentally impaired, disadvantaged. We just feel strongly about some of those areas. If the organizations have a Christian bent to them, that's very important to us, too. So there're some of these filtering processes." (Luke Z.). "We get about five donation requests a day—well we as a family. I think the first screen is a Christian cause; a second screen would be education, developmentally disabled, and those kinds of things; and then a third screen would probably have to do with getting the message out. We put about eighty percent of our money in education: Christian schools, Christian colleges." (Peter B.). "I feel I want to be a part of spreading the Gospel as much as I can. I give to Christian causes, Christian colleges, Christian schools, mission, building Christian leadership." (James M.).

Quite a number of CEOs donate to political causes—and to political candidates—often in combination with Christian missions. "We are trying to focus a bit more on some political activity and involvement. Politics has been for us an area of passion; we think that public policy and the political world should be one [that] Christians should speak in, not run away from. So my wife and I have both been involved in that. Education is another passion. We support many Christian and faith-based causes, and we like to keep about half our giving to organizations that have a very specific Christian mission and message. But about half of our giving is to organizations that may not have a specific Christian message. But execute a Christian mission." (Dale Z.).

Successful Dutch-American entrepreneurs give substantially to their churches, schools, and communities. Undoubtedly some of them also contribute to causes and support organizations they preferred not to mention, or rather, not have published. But they fully engage in the culture of giving, and their charitable donations are grounded in biblical doctrines of sharing. Charity is big in West Michigan, and the donations by Dutch-American CEOs are impressive.

Politics and Civic Involvement

West Michigan has a strong Republican vote. Its public image clearly mirrors this political preference. If we take Ottawa County—the county where Holland is located—as an example, President Bush received 71 percent of the vote during the 2000 general election, he got 72 percent of the vote in the 2004 election, and McCain drew 62 percent of the vote in the 2008 presidential election.[3] Already in 1928 renowned Dutch immigrant researcher Jacob Van Hinte observed: "The majority of the Dutch colonists became Republicans . . . and still is."[4] Politically West Michigan is conservative, and its many Reformed residents are no exception.[5] As we will see, this holds for Dutch-American CEOs as well.

---

[3]   Michigan Department of State, Bureau of Elections.

[4]   Jacob Van Hinte, *Netherlanders in America*, editor's introduction, xxxi. Van Hinte adds: "This final state of affairs in politics finds its most profound explanation perhaps in the Calvinism of these immigrants, coupled with their ethnic characteristics, a Calvinism that was aristocratically colored, primarily through its teachings of predestination," 443.

[5]   We lack data on the voting behavior of RCA and CRC members. But surveys indicate that 60 percent of RCA members and 73 percent of CRC members label themselves as politically conservative. Schmidt et al. conclude on the basis of these and comparable data that "the overall pattern . . . is that both the CRC and RCA are generally conservative politically, both at the lay and at the clergy level." Corwin Smidt, Donald Luidens, James Penning, and Roger Nemeth, *Divided by a Common Heritage. The Christian Reformed Church and the Reformed Church in America at the Beginning of the New Millennium* (Grand Rapids, MI/Cambridge, UK: Eerdmans, 2006), 131.

The Reformed tradition has always stressed the importance of political and social engagement. Abraham Kuyper (1837-1920), the personification of Dutch Neo-Calvinism, vigorously and relentlessly argued that Calvinism penetrates "every sphere of life," inasmuch as it is an encompassing life-and-world view. All human activity is subject to God's will and authority. Engagement, not withdrawal, is the Christian calling.[6] Dutch-American CEOs certainly do a fair share of civic engagement. On an aggregated basis, entrepreneurs interviewed in this study listed an impressive number of board memberships that reveal very active community involvement: Christian schools, Christian colleges, Christian seminaries, hospitals, museums, charity funds, volunteer organizations, environmental and nature conservation organizations, special interest foundations, health care, family care, care of the elderly, youth programs, downtown revitalization, oversees missions, and, of course, their churches and congregations. They spend a good deal of their time on community involvement. They do well at networking, which is of course also inspired by business interests. The vast majority of the Dutch-American entrepreneurs that participated in my study know one another well, either from business, boards, or charity and, of course, from church. Quite a few are related by family ties. In this section I will explore political views and party preference of the CEOs. I am especially interested in the way they believe a preference for the Republican Party, conservative political views and traditional moral convictions (such as pro life) are interrelated, and whether this pattern is characteristic for the West Michigan political climate in general and for successful Dutch-American entrepreneurs in particular.

For some CEOs, being active in politics is not merely a question of advancing a political agenda but is also a Christian assignment that transcends current affairs and the issues of today. "It's a part of the Reformed world view, we are a part of the world. And the world is not just business, not in my view. We are citizens, stewards of a much broader perspective." (Dale Z.). "Your responsibility is to use all of your skills for the furtherance of the Kingdom. That's just the way it is. You can go back to Kuyper, but it's true." (Mark F.). Quite a few CEOs affirm that most successful Dutch-American entrepreneurs share Republican political views, pro-life beliefs, and conservative family values. "I think that there are a lot of Dutch conservative people in this area, and I think that they have become very involved in voicing their opinions,

[6]   Abraham Kuyper, *Lectures on Calvinism*, (Grand Rapids, MI: Eerdmans, 1931, [ninth printing, 1976]). See also James D. Bratt, *Dutch Calvinism in Modern America. A History of a Conservative Subculture* (Grand Rapids, MI/Cambridge, UK: Eerdmans, 1984).

to promote this conservative agenda." (Gene H.). "I think it's the congruence of economic and social conservatism in this community, a confluence of entrepreneurship and faith." (Dale Z.). "This is one of the most Republican areas of the country, so it probably aligns with that conservatism's frugalness so that there is probably alignment there." (Harry V.). "I think there's a sense of individual responsibility in this community that leads you toward a more conservative direction. I think it's pretty Biblical—a pro-life position is Biblical. The responsibility to govern—all the issues are: give to Caesar what's Caesar's, but give to God what's God's. And then there's just a huge sense of taking care of yourself as far as hard work, and of course, the safety net is huge, that's our churches and the way we live. I think that just lends itself toward those political feelings. It's an extraordinary Reformed, Dutch Reformed community." (Mark F.).

For most CEOs, the Republican Party is the obvious party of their choice and preference. "I'm a conservative Republican. I want less taxes, less government. I believe in life, liberty, and the pursuit of happiness." (Albert I.). "Business men who are not Republicans, I don't frankly understand. How a business person could advocate an economic world view that is completely at odds with the way they have to run their business is surprising. I think that a business person, a thoughtful business person, leads you to a Republican world view, a view of free trade, a view of appropriate free markets." (Dale Z.). "I'm certainly a Republican, but more than that, I consider myself conservative. I'm a little cautious when it comes to political labels. I'm not as strong a Republican as some of the others, but that still is my political background. I believe in smaller government rather than greater, allowing people to make decisions themselves rather than someone else making decisions for them. That is why I am not so crazy about some of the European models." (Chris G.). "Well, I am not an Obama man. He is the president, and quite honestly we pray for the president to do a good job, we don't pray for president Obama's policies, we do pray for him to do a good job. He is a man in authority, and we are taught to respect the people in authority. But I am not an Obama man, oh man oh man, we need to get him out of there, it's really costing us; we have some bad things happening to us." (Peter B.). "The Republicans are much closer to what I believe as far as pro-life and the whole gay agenda that has in the last fifteen years moved to where it's to the point where this is normal, this is . . . and a lot of lies. I just don't want an agenda like that pushed especially upon young children when they're growing up" (James M.).

Some CEOs take a more moderate political stand. "I probably don't represent that extremely Republican conservatism. I am more of a moderate. I get to listen to a lot of different ideas, and I am trying to get people to come together and work collaboratively as opposed to taking strong positions and creating conflict." (Harry V.). "I grew up in that background and I am Republican by philosophy, but I find that I am disassociating myself with Republicanism to the point that it has been hard for me to hang the American flag on the fourth of July, because I didn't want to be associated with the Republicanism of torture and violating of the Geneva convention and the Bill of Rights. I am a little troubled resolving that with the Calvinistic principles, which is caring for people in general. And I never thought I would lean to the left, I always thought I was pretty conservative, but I find myself falling into the left camp, and I am not sure if I got more liberal or the world and everyone around me has taken two steps to the right and I was left standing where I was." (Jerry V.). "I'm probably not as far right as some; maybe a little bit more in the middle. I probably share more from a value standpoint and beliefs line up with Republicans, but I'm not a staunch Republican—much more independent in that way than a lot. I hope that Obama's able to accomplish some things that might never have been accomplished before. I'm hopeful that Obama's legacy is that he offers a different path and vision for a lot of folks within the African-American community. I think it's one of our biggest problems in this country, the situation of the African-American community." (Jeff C.). Also here, there is a generational issue. "If you looked at my dad's generation, then you can pretty easily characterize that as Republican, conservative across almost all issues; that's the way it is. Across my generation, I would describe myself as conservative on fiscal and financial issues. I have a pretty conservative philosophy on jobs and those things. On social issues I would describe myself as more moderate to liberal. Such as on welfare issues. Some folks just need help." (Luke Z.).

Some CEOs question the relevance of the Republican-Democrat political dichotomy and feel America should go back to basics. "I don't necessarily think it's all bad, but you see for me, I never needed that. So I am not a Democrat, but I preach this, we are all Americans, let's stop this Republican/Democrat business for tomorrow; it's for the birds. I get rid of a lot of that. I think it's all baloney. Get back to the basics of religion." (Victor H.).

The general picture in the political domain is that successful Dutch-American entrepreneurs feel a strong bond with the Republican Party, particularly with respect to its conservative economic agenda and for many its stands on moral issues. The choice for the Republican Party is almost unanimous. But behind this Republican preference there is variation according to support for different political branches and positions in the political specter. Dutch-American entrepreneurs are Republicans, but not all of them are staunch Republicans.

CHAPTER 8

The Calvinist Credo and the Spirit of Capitalism: Conclusions and Perspective

We believe that practicing compassionate capitalism is the secret to real financial success.

Rich DeVos
Compassionate Capitalism (1993)

In his classic and highly influential study *Democracy in America* (1835, 1840), Alexis de Tocqueville (1805-1859) described the American spirit of capitalism as the restless activity of Americans to make a profit by working hard. Profit seeking is an honorable pursuit in American culture. The American spirit of enterprise according to this eminent nineteenth century French political philosopher, historian, and statesman is fueled by a sense of restiveness, a [contained] love for material well-being, and a certain audacity or courage in business. Tocqueville argues that this "boldness of enterprise is the foremost cause of [America's] rapid progress, its strength and its greatness."[1]

Dutch-American entrepreneurs certainly had and have their share of entrepreneurial boldness. West Michigan—the focus of this study—with its high concentration of Dutch immigrants shows a

---

[1] Alexis de Tocqueville, *Democracy in America* (New York/Toronto: Alfred A. Knopf, 1994), part 2, 236. See also Richard Swedberg, "Tocqueville and the Spirit of American Capitalism," Cornell University, Center for the Study of Economy & Society (CSES), Ithaca, NY, 2004 and his recent book *Tocqueville's Political Economy* (Princeton, NJ: Princeton University Press, 2009).

remarkable number of vibrant and flourishing companies founded by Dutch-American entrepreneurs. Several of these companies developed into extraordinarily successful family-operated mega businesses with an economic radius far beyond the state of Michigan. Many Dutch-American entrepreneurs did and do well. Is there a cultural secret to their success? Do successful Dutch-American businessmen share cultural capital characteristics that facilitate entrepreneurship, for example, in terms of their ethnic heritage, their religious values, and their community ties? Is Dutch-American entrepreneurial boldness the result of a unique cultural combination of faith, family, and fortune? Do Dutch-American businessmen perceive the impact of their Dutch heritage and their Reformed upbringing and beliefs on their success as an innovative entrepreneur?

To answer these intriguing questions, I interviewed more than twenty outstandingly successful (present and former) Dutch-American CEOs in West Michigan. Some of them lead companies with an annual turnover of several billion dollars. This book reports the main findings. In this final chapter, I summarize the results, present the main conclusions, and put them into perspective.

It is important to make a methodological qualification. The group of Dutch-American CEOs I interviewed for this book is not a random sample. They have been selected on the basis of their remarkable success as businessmen. Dutch-American entrepreneurs that failed are not part of the study. In methodological terms this implies a (self) selection effect: only highly effective entrepreneurs were invited to participate. But the findings are exemplary for the group of outstanding Dutch-American entrepreneurs.

The first issue we need to address is how salient the adjective *Dutch* is in the cultural triangle of religion, heritage, and entrepreneurial success. The interviews clearly indicate that excelling Dutch-American CEOs regard their Dutch background in overwhelmingly positive terms. They share a common ethnic identity, a sense of cultural belonging, and an awareness of being part of a value-based community. They believe that their ethnic heritage is a defining part of their family's immigration history and that this heritage reflects essential religious, personal, and social values. Moreover, they believe that the history and achievements of the Netherlands transcend the smallness of the country, particularly in terms of its political, cultural, and economic significance. In short: successful Dutch-American entrepreneurs positively identify with their ethnic legacy.

Ethnic identification with their Dutch roots is important to Dutch-American CEOs, *but* religious identification with the underlying

Reformed teachings and morals is of much greater weight. Being part of the Calvinist tradition is much more determining for their self-understanding and identity than their Dutch descent. They certainly cherish their Dutchness and treasure their roots, but their ethnic affection and attachment is to some degree primarily metaphoric. Being of Dutch extraction generates feelings of pride and fondness, but it does not determine their existential "self." The Dutch roots of Dutch-American entrepreneurs help to understand their family history, but their Reformed faith, religion, and churches shape and justify their personal identity. Dutch-American entrepreneurs are first and foremost *American* entrepreneurs.

Faith, so the conclusion holds, is more relevant than ethnicity. But given the peculiar immigration history of the Dutch presence in West Michigan, being Dutch-American in most cases simply implied being Reformed or Christian Reformed. In such a cultural and religious context, it is nearly impossible to separate the ethnic and religious dimension: they mirror two sides of the same phenomenon. In this context ethnicity and religion are interlinked. But on a relative scale, religion evidently is the more important part of the cultural equation. On a more general level, it has been argued that the stronger the religious identity of an immigrant group, the less it needs an explicit ethnic or national identity.[2] This hypothesis seems to apply quite well to the Dutch-American community.

It is critical to underline that metaphoric ethnic identification does not equal ethnic superficiality by pointing at what Herbert Gans has labeled "symbolic ethnicity."[3] This form of ethnic identification, Gans writes, "is characterized by a nostalgic allegiance to the culture of the immigrant generation, or that of the old country; a love for and a pride in a tradition that can be felt without having to be incorporated into everyday behavior."[4] It is there, but it does not direct one's personal life. Symbolic ethnicity, other studies show, is typical for many Dutch-American communities.[5] Religious identification, however, does affect all domains of CEOs' existence and determines how they view the world and their role in it. Being part of the Reformed tradition with its all-embracing Calvinist beliefs and values models their self-understanding and identity.

Dutch-American entrepreneurs' upbringing clearly echoed the comprehensive and overpowering influence of Reformed doctrine and

---

[2] Cf. Hans Krabbendam, *Freedom on the Horizon*, 333.
[3] Herbert J. Gans, "Symbolic Ethnicity," 193-220.
[4] Gans, 436.
[5] See Peter Ester, *Growing up Dutch-American*, 2007.

norms. All CEOs state that the Reformed teachings as they were passed on during their formative period—their youth years—by their parents, their family, their school, their church, and their community, taught them responsibility, obedience, hard work, sharing, and the need for structure and rules. The pattern was transparent and self-explanatory: you lead a Christian lifestyle, you attend church, you work hard, you take care of yourself, your family, and your property, you spend money carefully, and you treat others respectfully. These vital moral lessons, according to my CEO sample, were instilled in them and became a major pillar of their career as a businessman. The Reformed teachings markedly affected their biography and career as well as their outlook on society and the world.

Ethnicity as such may be less salient among Dutch-American CEOs, but family is very significant. Most of the companies founded by my respondents are family businesses. Marriage and family are core social institutions in the Reformed world. Tocqueville also recognized the key role played by these institutions in American society, and the way this role is sanctioned by religion. "There is certainly no country in the world where the tie of marriage is more respected than in America or where conjugal happiness is more highly or worthily appreciated. The American derives from his own home that love of order which he afterwards carries with him into public affairs."[6] A healthy family life plays an important role in economic life, Tocqueville states, and it is an essential part of an entrepreneurial economy. "When the American retires from the turmoil of public life to the bosom of his family, he finds in it the image of order and of peace. There his pleasures are simple and natural, his joys are innocent and calm, and as he finds that an orderly life is the surest path to happiness, he accustoms himself easily to moderate his opinions as well as his tastes."[7] Family companies are not idyllic businesses, inasmuch as they create their own micro-dynamics, for example, in respect to family conflicts, malfunctioning family members, or the always pressing issue of leadership succession. But some of the Dutch-American enterprises in West Michigan manage to have a substantial number of family members on board.[8] This requires permanent fine tuning of the delicate balance of the family agenda and the business agenda.

Tocqueville found Americans to be very religious: "there is no country in the world where the Christian religion retains a greater

[6]   Alexis de Tocqueville, *Democracy in America*, part 1, 304.
[7]   Ibid., part 1, 304.
[8]   See DeVos, *Compassionate Capitalism*, 234.

influence over the souls of men than in America, and there can be no greater proof of its utility and of its conformity to human nature than that its influence is powerfully felt over the most enlightened and free nation of the earth."[9] He was particularly impressed by the role of religion in America in the economic realm. Religion teaches individuals focus, method, and structure in their pursuit of economic goals. Through religion, individuals learn how to limit their otherwise endless desires and how to face everyday temptations. Religion teaches higher rewards beyond the here and now. The emphasis on religion as a factor that limits infinite desires is interesting, because it implies a primary focus on desires that can or need to be satisfied. And it is exactly at this point that entrepreneurship enters Tocqueville's reasoning: providing products to satisfy needs through a methodical and structured approach.[10] The Puritan ethic is a central notion in how Tocqueville relates religion to the spirit of American capitalism, particularly in the way it values good morals, order, and work as an honorable activity. He emphasizes the unique union of religion and freedom as the core of American civilization and its spirit of capitalism: "The Americans are at the same time a puritanical and a commercial nation."[11]

The values and beliefs underlying this coalition of Puritanism and entrepreneurship are very characteristic of the doctrines and morals that Dutch-American CEOs were socialized in during their youth years. Indeed, Puritanism and Reformed thought show many resemblances. The work ethic, taking responsibility for one's actions, meeting expectations, discipline, moderation, time consciousness, loyalty, honesty and integrity, respect and obedience, attending church and Sunday observance were clear and non-negotiable values and rules when Dutch-American entrepreneurs were young. In many cases the nature of their upbringing was rather strict. Overt rebellion among CEOs was rare. Reformed faith and Reformed doctrine made up the belief system in and by which Dutch-American entrepreneurs were firmly socialized. The church (Reformed or Christian Reformed) was the community bastion *par excellence* that guarded theological doctrine, prescribed everyday rules of conduct, demanded discipline and structure, offered meaning and comfort, and exercised social control. It was the authoritative social institution in Dutch-American communities, but at the same time provided identity and cohesion.

---

[9]   Alexis de Tocqueville, *Democracy in America*, part 1, 303-4.
[10] See Swedberg, "Tocqueville and the Spirit of American Capitalism."
[11] Tocqueville, *Democracy in America*, part 1, 201.

My sample of highly successful entrepreneurs shares vivid memories of how church life influenced their youth, and they are quite outspoken on how this affected their later business career. Reformed values and principles had a major influence on the way Dutch-American CEOs built and developed their company. Their reports include accountability, honesty, fairness, discipline, patience, perseverance, trust, and work ethos as prime examples of the impact of the Reformed worldview. They all admit that their entrepreneurship greatly benefited from this firm Calvinist credo. Their Reformed upbringing taught them elementary standards that guided their career as a moral compass. It also taught them a set of disciplined behaviors that were extremely helpful in their later career and career choices. The worldly business success of Reformed Dutch-American entrepreneurs has solid roots in their resolute Calvinist socialization. The strict values, norms, and morals that shepherded their youth prepared them well—so our CEOs stress—for their career as an entrepreneur. Their Reformed upbringing highlighted typical abilities that turned out to be distinctive qualities for adept entrepreneurship.

Tocqueville greatly admired Americans for their entrepreneurial spirit: "I cannot better explain my meaning than by saying that the Americans show a sort of heroism in their manner of trading. . . . America is a land of wonders, in which everything is in a constant motion, and every change seems an improvement. The idea of novelty is there indissolubly connected with the idea of amelioration. No natural boundary seems to be set to the efforts of man; and in his eyes what is not yet done is only what he has not yet attempted to do."[12] The American entrepreneurial spirit according to Tocqueville is to vigorously explore new challenges, to try new approaches, and to imagine a better future. The entrepreneur's mission is "to be a man of singular warmth in his desires, enterprising, fond of adventure and, above all, of novelty."[13] This passionate spirit is not only characteristic for the world of commerce but also typifies the domain of religion, the law, and politics.

Trading is, Tocqueville observed, almost a second nature of Americans: "[they] are constantly driven to engage in commerce and industry. Their origin, their social conditions, their political institutions, and even the region they inhabit urge them irresistibly in this direction. Their present condition, then, is that of an almost exclusively manufacturing and commercial association, placed in the

---

[12]   Ibid., part 1, 424-25.
[13]   Ibid., part 1, 426.

midst of a new and boundless country, which their principal object is to explore for purposes of profit."[14]

Dutch-American CEOs can easily relate to Tocqueville's description—written in 1831—of the American entrepreneurial spirit. Though we know from the literature (chapter two) that there are no singular personality traits that unequivocally distinguish successful entrepreneurs from non-successful ones, there are some personal qualities that Dutch-American CEOs single out. You have to have a bright and innovative business idea with clear market potential, the idea should be framed within a broader creative vision on changing market needs, and the business opportunity should be seized at the right moment. The combination of an innovative idea, vision, opportunity, and timing is essential. The successful entrepreneur selects the right people to develop his business; he remains focused on the creative vision, and builds his company with hard work, perseverance, and concentration. Discipline, anticipation, and preparation for bad times are critical too. He (or she) has the right values and leadership skills to turn innovation into business and to sustain the business vision. The successful entrepreneur is persistent but must also have a keen eye for a good balance between determination and the proactive willingness to adjust to changing external conditions. A gifted entrepreneur needs talent but must also be willing to work long hours. Moreover, talented businessmen are often role models for other entrepreneurs and are active members of their community.

Most of these entrepreneurial qualities were (directly or indirectly) reinforced by the principles and values Dutch-American entrepreneurs were taught in their formative period. Talent development, focus, commitment, persistence, work ethic, responsibility, accountability, discipline, preparation, and structure are basic personal qualities that are stressed in the Reformed tradition. These qualities, of course, are not exclusive features of the Reformed faith that set it apart from other denominations, but my respondents experienced an intrinsic and close bond between their success as an entrepreneur and their Reformed upbringing.

It is not just a case of the right personal qualities, however, that make a difference. Several CEOs describe the process of building their company as a journey, almost in the Mosaic sense. It is a journey full of challenges, pitfalls, temptations, victories and defeats, prosperity

---

[14]   Tocqueville, *Democracy in America*, part 2, 235.

and hardship, fortune and failure. Their faith helped them in this business cycle of good times and bad times. It provided comfort and taught them patience and perseverance. It also gave them new energy, prospects, and hope. Faith consoles and reassures. Their faith gave Dutch-American businessmen strength to continue their journey as an entrepreneur. Again, one needs to emphasize that this effect of faith is not a case of Reformed exceptionalism, but their faith evidently helped Dutch-American entrepreneurs through the different and sometimes very difficult stages of their business career.

Calculated risk-taking, as I discussed extensively in chapter two, is a chief if not *the* major dimension of the entrepreneur's business calculus. Proficient entrepreneurs are effective risk takers. They see opportunities, they weigh the pros and cons, and then they act. Tocqueville described risk-taking as a quality that distinguishes American businessmen from their European counterparts. "The whole life of an American is passed like a game of chance, a revolutionary crisis, or a battle."[15] The stakes are high. Risk-taking, so Tocqueville observed, is a fundamental feature of American culture and entrepreneurship. "Commercial business is there [in America] like a vast lottery. . . . But any bold speculation risks the fortune of the speculator and of all those who put their trust in him. The Americans, who make a virtue of commercial temerity, have no right in any case to brand with disgrace those who practice it. Hence arises the strange indulgence that is shown to bankrupts in the United States; their honor does not suffer by such an accident."[16]

Dutch-American CEOs agree that calculated risk-taking is the central quality of a successful entrepreneur. Without risk-taking, there is no entrepreneurship. They stress, however, that it is calculated risk, not gambling. In reality, though, in many situations the line between calculable and non-calculable risks is a thin one. Though in most cases risk-taking is determined first and foremost by economic conditions and financial circumstances, it is interesting how Dutch-American entrepreneurs interpret the role of personal faith in addressing the issue of business risks. Faith reduces fears and provides comfort. It gives confidence and trust. Faith frames destiny in a different way and offers existential certainty; it presents a theodicy that helps to explain the human condition. Moreover, faith provides a time horizon that transcends the here and now. It structures short-term decision making in a broader time perspective. The future lies in the hands of their

[15]   Ibid., part 1, 426.
[16]   Ibid., part 2, 236.

Creator; God takes care of their lives. Entrepreneurs indicate that their faith greatly helped them in hard times when the company's future was at stake, when they had to make tough decisions and had to radically redefine their business strategy—often with great risks involved.

Several CEOs relate risk-taking to emigration. Leaving the old country and starting a new life in a new, unknown country implies taking great risks by emigrants and their families. Emigration is a risky act and an act of risks. To build a new existence in a strange land requires extensive risk-taking. Their faith and religion were the prime weapons by which Calvinist Dutch emigrants addressed the substantial risks that confronted them in their new country.

Is there a unique and recognizable way in which Reformed values and principles play a role in which Dutch-American companies treat their customers and employees? Some companies do indeed have a mission statement that makes explicit their core Christian values and beliefs. This typically depends on the degree of outspokenness of the company's CEO on this issue. But most companies operate in a more indirect and implicit way, that is, without an identifiable reference to their Reformed roots. Quality, fair treatment, respect, trust, honesty, and integrity are the main values mentioned by Dutch-American CEOs when characterizing their customer and personnel policy. Personally, CEOs do refer to the Reformed tradition and their Dutch heritage as the main sources for stressing these elementary values but do not communicate them in this specific way to their customers or to their employees. Thus, the degree of linking policies to faith and heritage varies with the stands and personality of the individual CEO. Some of them are very upfront and open in this respect, but most of them prefer a more subtle and general approach.[17]

Do Dutch-American CEOs themselves believe that being of Dutch extraction and sharing the Reformed faith helped other Dutch-American entrepreneurs as well in building their companies? Do they see that successful Dutch-American entrepreneurs have particular values and skills in common? Do they see parallels? Though the ethnic component has a somewhat ambivalent place in the picture, Dutch-American CEOs point to the beneficial combination in West Michigan of a risk-taking culture, a can-do and solution oriented mentality, a value

[17]   Corrie Mazereeuw-van der Duijn Schouten, *Doing Business for Heaven's Sake*, found a somewhat complex pattern of relationships between Dutch executives' traditional religiosity and socially responsible business conduct (SRBC). Religiosity has a direct positive influence on charity but a negative influence on SRBC in terms of diversity issues. Otherwise, religiosity has only indirect influences.

system that favors responsibility and commitment, and a distinctive work ethos. This culture of Calvinism, character, and commitment is, according to my sample of leading Dutch-American entrepreneurs, a solid and competitive foundation for excellent entrepreneurship. It is a cultural combination that makes an economic difference.

Americans love wealth, so Tocqueville claims. In fact American society is all about material well-being. Their love of wealth is directly linked to the American project of conquering the boundless land. "To clear, to till, and to transform the vast uninhabited continent which is his domain, the American requires the daily support of an energetic passion; that passion can only be the love of wealth; the passion for wealth is therefore not reprobated in America . . . it is held in honor."[18] The passion for material goods and comfort, for prosperity and progress is, according to Tocqueville, a national characteristic of America and related to its immigration history, which accentuates a longing for improvement and security. "The love of well-being has now become the predominant taste of the nation; the great current of human passions runs in that channel and sweeps everything along its course."[19] The passion for wealth has created a restless culture of hedonism, of instant gratification, of an impulsive and almost "sad" search for new pleasures. "A native of the United States clings to this world's goods as if he were certain never to die; and he is so hasty in grasping at all within his reach that one would suppose he was constantly afraid of not living long enough to enjoy them."[20] It appears, so Tocqueville argues, that the Puritan ethos has been replaced by a consumer ethos. Even religion mirrors this restless search for gratification, to a degree that it is often difficult to ascertain "whether the principal object of religion is to procure eternal felicity in the other world or prosperity in this."[21]

The entrepreneurs participating in this study are all well-to-do. Some of them are even very wealthy. Their affluence is a direct effect of their success in business. They built prosperous and profitable companies for which they received all the material and immaterial rewards. Do they see a tension between the emphasis within the

---

[18]   Alexis de Tocqueville, *Democracy in America*, part 2, 236.
[19]   Ibid., part 2, 130.
[20]   Ibid., part 2, 136.
[21]   Ibid., part 2, 127. But Tocqueville also states that religion has a mitigating effect on the pursuit of wealth: "men wish to be as well off as they can in this world without forgoing their chance of another." Excesses are to be avoided. The passion for materialistic enjoyment may be universal "but its range is confined. To build enormous palaces, to conquer or to mimic nature, to ransack the world in order to gratify the passions of a man, is not thought of," part 2, 132.

Reformed tradition on frugality and simplicity and the lifestyle they lead? And if so, how do they personally justify or solve this discrepancy? How do they reconcile faith and fortune? I need to emphasize that the highly successful Dutch-American entrepreneurs I interviewed lead quite different lifestyles. Some are not afraid to show their wealth and material success; others are much more reluctant in exhibiting worldly goods. Some demonstrate their affluence; others prefer a much more modest way of life. Among the latter, one observes the classic Reformed habit of material prudence and reservation. One even notices a traditional Dutch cultural element here: the value of thrift. Thus, both lifestyle extremes (hedonism and modesty) can be found among highly successful Dutch-American CEOs. But asceticism in the classic Weberian sense, let alone *Reformed* asceticism in the Troeltschian meaning, is no longer discernible among Dutch-American entrepreneurs.[22]

Almost indistinguishably, CEOs attribute their wealth and success to God's grace. Their affluence is defined as a blessing from the Almighty. This reference both explains and legitimizes their material prosperity. Their success in business is not justified as the mere result of their entrepreneurial talents, their hard work, or their profitable risk-taking, but as a sign of the grace of God. The interviews show that entrepreneurs almost automatically refer to this traditional Reformed interpretation. Interestingly, some CEOs spontaneously admit that this theologically correct Calvinist response is somewhat gratuitous, and comes easily. Whatever their lifestyle is, there are no mutually disapproving feelings among well-to-do Dutch-American entrepreneurs that favor different ways of life. They grant their fellow entrepreneurs their success because they know the efforts it takes to build and lead a company.

Perhaps more interesting than these lifestyle observations is that all CEOs affirm the great responsibility that wealth implies: the need for giving and sharing. And here we meet another deeply rooted American phenomenon: the amazing culture of philanthropy among affluent Americans. In this respect, too, Tocqueville's observations and interpretations of American society are helpful. He states that the principle of enlightened self-interest guides Americans' lives but not by excluding pro-social behavior or the interests of others. Americans are able to balance individualism with notions of community. The American doctrine of enlightened self-interest combines individualistic

[22] See Emma de Ruiter, "People, Product, Progress," 1999, for observations on the loss of the frugal lifestyle that was characteristic for orthodox Calvinist groups in Zeeland, MI.

and altruistic goals. "Each American knows when to sacrifice some of his private interests to save the rest. . . . They show with complacency how an enlightened regard for themselves constantly prompts them to assist one another and inclines them willingly to sacrifice a portion of their time and property."[23] Christianity, in Tocqueville's view, plays a crucial role in advancing the doctrine of enlightened self-interest. "Christianity, indeed, teaches that a man must prefer his neighbor to himself in order to gain eternal life; but Christianity also teaches that men ought to benefit their fellow creatures for the love of God. A sublime expression!"[24] Rational self-interest and doing good are not antagonistic categories. Self-interest and giving go together well in American society.

As we described in the introduction, Dutch-American entrepreneurs interviewed for this book have a tremendous track record of giving to their communities, their churches, their schools, and to a wide array of charities. The amount of money they spend on good causes is truly amazing. West Michigan cities and towns provide visible proof of the generosity of Dutch-American entrepreneurs. They have donated substantial sums of money to hospitals, museums, schools, colleges and universities, education grants, disabled groups, nature conservation, environmental projects, urban revitalization, performing arts, and numerous other causes. Dutch-American CEOs give, and they give profusely. Through their charitable foundations they contribute many, many millions of dollars. Enlightened self-interest is surely an important explanation but particularly in the Reformed version: tithing.[25] Many of my respondents mentioned that tithing—giving one-tenth of one's earnings as a voluntary contribution to church—was a rule that was observed in their youth by their parents. It was a moral obligation to give and to share. In their adult life Dutch-American entrepreneurs honored this traditional Reformed duty to provide for, but on a much larger and broader scale.

My respondents are major sponsors of charity projects and philanthropic initiatives. But they are also otherwise active in their communities. They hold positions in their churches, serve on community committees, help raise money for good causes, and

---

[23]   Alexis de Tocqueville, *Democracy in America*, part 2, 122.

[24]   Ibid., part 2, 125.

[25]   There is also, of course, a much broader explanation of the wide diffusion of the culture of charity in America: compared to European welfare states, the role of the government is much more limited in providing collective goods such as welfare, social security or education. The role of market forces and private initiative are politically more accentuated in American history and society.

participate in volunteer organizations. Their motivation to be involved in community programs is, for most of them, a combination of their religious beliefs and of their business interests. CEOs state that they are often asked by their business friends to contribute their time and talent. Here too, one sees the principle of enlightened self-interest. Tocqueville was one of the first foreign observers who reflected on the importance of volunteering in American society. He recognized and applauded Americans' involvement in civil action. Americans are joiners, observes Tocqueville: "Americans of all ages, all conditions, and all dispositions constantly form associations." He observes wide networks that included "not only commercial and manufacturing companies, in which all take part, but associations of a thousand other kinds, religious, moral, serious, futile, general or restricted, enormous or diminutive. The Americans, make associations to give entertainments, to found seminaries, to build inns, to construct churches, to diffuse books, to send missionaries to the antipodes; in this manner they found hospitals, prisons, and schools."[26] In a later stage of the social sciences, Tocqueville's notions on volunteering and civic engagement in American society would become elementary ingredients of theories on civil society and social capital.[27] The civic involvement of Dutch-American CEOs can be seen as part of this distinctive "participant civic culture" and commitment to public affairs.[28] Their civic engagement is rooted in this tradition of the American civil model, which also stresses the civic obligation of successful entrepreneurs to participate in volunteering to advance the common good. It is an obligation that is well founded in the Reformed tradition too.[29]

Tocqueville, like my respondents, was an ardent adherent of free trade and free business enterprise. He, moreover, was a dedicated opponent of bureaucracy and of an almighty state. As a liberal—in the European meaning of the concept—and as an anti-revolutionary political thinker, he strongly believed in freedom which, he describes as a "sacred thing." Freedom is not shallow self-interest but explicitly refers to the common good and to personal virtue. Free enterprise is the

---

[26] Alexis de Tocqueville, *Democracy in America*, part 2, 106.

[27] Robert D. Putnam, *Bowling Alone: The Collapse and Revival of American Community* (New York: Simon & Schuster, 2000). See also Peter Ester and Henk Vinken, "Debating Civil Society," in *International Sociology* 18 (2003): 659-80. Thea Skocpol and Morris P. Fiorina, eds. *Civic Engagement in American Democracy* (Washington, DC: Brookings Institution Press, New York: Russell Sage Foundation, 1999).

[28] Gabriel Almond and Sidney Verba, *The Civic Culture: Political Attitudes and Democracy in Five Nations* (Princeton, NJ: Princeton University Press, 1963).

[29] See, e.g., James D. Bratt, *Dutch Calvinism in Modern America*.

best economic and political system to advance common interests and individual morality. "I know of nothing more opposite to revolutionary attitudes than commercial ones. Commerce is naturally adverse to all the violent passions; it loves to temporize, takes delight in compromise and studiously avoids irritation. It is patient, insinuating, flexible, and never has recourse to extreme measures until obliged by the most absolute necessity. Commerce renders men independent of one another, gives them a lofty notion of their personal importance, leads them to seek to conduct their own affairs, and teaches them how to conduct well; it therefore prepares men for freedom, but preserves them from revolutions."[30] In Tocqueville's perspective, free enterprise does not equal naked self-interest but requires a context of morality, of virtue. The world of commerce should not operate outside the world of ethics.

Free enterprise, evidently, is a cornerstone of Dutch-American entrepreneurs' political beliefs. They are all firm supporters of this fundamental capitalist axiom and passionately defend its virtuousness and blessings. There appears to be little intellectual sensitivity to other political and economic paradigms. Capitalist axioms are not subject to criticism, for example, in terms of external effects such as inequality, environmental impact, or consumerism. Capitalism is good. It therefore does not come as a surprise that Dutch-American CEOs embrace Republican convictions and values. Most of them have voted for the Republican Party all of their lives. Free enterprise, non-interference of the state in economic and private affairs, selective and controlled government spending, and anti-bureaucracy are topics that unite Dutch-American entrepreneurs. But they also share conservative stands on moral issues, for example, on vetoing abortion and gay marriage. The combined conservative economic and pro-life moral agenda is what CEOs bind to the Republican Party. This choice is practically unanimous. But given this preference there is room for variation in political beliefs. Dutch-American entrepreneurs, certainly, support the Republican Party but they are not uncritical voters. It is hard to find a liberal Dutch-American CEO, but this does not imply that all of them are servile Republicans.

Calvinism and capitalism, to conclude, are close friends as far as Dutch-American entrepreneurs are concerned. The basic premises go well together, both in terms of doctrine, mores, and worldview. Or as Jay Van Andel—the icon of Dutch-American entrepreneurship—states in his autobiography: "I believe free enterprise works best when guided

---

[30]   Alexis de Tocqueville, *Democracy in America*, part 2, 254.

by traditional Judeo-Christian principles."[31] Excellency of Dutch-American entrepreneurship is shaped by a unique cultural fusion of the Calvinist ethos and the capitalist spirit reinforced by a supportive Dutch-American heritage. It is this cultural fusion that is still a dominant feature of the West Michigan economic landscape.

[31] Jay Van Andel, *An Enterprising Life*, 21.

Dutch-American Entrepreneurs Questionnaire[1]

Introduction

I would like to start by thanking you for this interview. My research is on the relationship between entrepreneurial success and personal religious beliefs, with a particular focus on Calvinism. West Michigan has a striking presence of successful Dutch-American enterprises or perhaps more accurately: enterprises founded or run by Dutch-Americans. Your enterprise is one of them. Several of these enterprises turned into mega businesses. Many of these successful Dutch-American entrepreneurs are active members of Reformed or Christian Reformed churches. This raises the question whether there is a link between Dutch-American upbringing, Reformed beliefs and values, and business success.

As a highly successful Dutch-American entrepreneur you are uniquely qualified to be interviewed in this study. The interview topics include how you look back on your Dutch-American upbringing, the

---

[1] For two interviewees an adjusted version of the questionnaire was used in view of their non-Reformed secular background.

beliefs and values you were taught, and whether you feel that these beliefs and values had an impact on your success as an entrepreneur. Is there a match, directly or indirectly, between the qualities of a successful entrepreneur and the beliefs and values of a Dutch-American upbringing and a Reformed or Christian Reformed view of man and society?

Everything you tell me is strictly confidential. No information will be used that can be linked to your person.

I would like to start with some personal facts.

Demographics

Name of Respondent
Date of Interview
Gender   O Male O Female
Age   _____ Years

Formal title of your position in the company

Is this the only company that you founded, or were there more entrepreneurial ventures that preceded this one? What were they, and how successful were they?

Church Affiliation

Church Affiliation of Parents

Marital status	O Married
	O Widowed
	O Divorced
	O Single
If not single, spouse Dutch-American?	O Yes O No
Does spouse work in company?	O Yes O No
Do you have children?	O Yes O No
Do some of your children work	O Yes _____ children
in your company?	O No

How many generations has your family been in America? For example, are you third, fourth, of fifth generation Dutch-American?

I am _____ generation Dutch-American.

Your Dutch Background

1. I would like to start with a more general question. How important is your Dutch background to you? Do you feel proud of it, or does it not matter to you at all?

Could you explain that to me?

Your Upbringing

2. When you were young, how did you first come to know your family was of Dutch heritage?

3. Did your parents make a point of teaching you about your family's Dutch background or was it merely taken for granted?

4. Were there any typical Dutch-American customs or manners that were part of your youth?

5. What were the main norms and values – apart from religious ones - that your parents taught you?

6. How would you characterize your upbringing: was it quite strict or more lenient?

7. What were absolutely forbidden, non- negotiable matters?

8. Were these norms and values pretty much the American standard in your youth or was there something typically Dutch-American about it?

Your Youth and the Church

9. How important was the church in your youth? Which role did the church play in everyday life?

10. What did a typical Sunday look like in your youth? How often did you go to church?

11. How did you feel as a young person about the main moral rules and regulations of the church?

12. Do you feel that your Dutch-American and (Christian) Reformed upbringing was a good basis for your later career as an entrepreneur?

Entrepreneurship

13. What in your view are the main qualities that make for a highly successful entrepreneur?

14. Are there personal characteristics that separate successful entrepreneurs from non-successful entrepreneurs?

15. You are a very successful entrepreneur. Do you feel that the norms and values you were taught in your youth had an impact on your success as an entrepreneur?

16. What are concrete examples in your career as an entrepreneur of this impact?

17. Were some of the more strategic choices of your company in any way related to your values and norms? Or are these choices solely based on economic and market arguments?

18. Do the values and norms that come from your Dutch-American and (Christian) Reformed upbringing influence how you want your company to come across to customers?

19. Is there a link between your personal values and norms and the personnel policies in your company?

20. Do you see the impact of being raised in a Dutch-American culture and the Reformed religion on other successful Dutch-American entrepreneurs as well?

21. Do successful Dutch-American entrepreneurs have certain characteristics in common? If so, which?

Entrepreneurs and personal life style

22. Your success as an entrepreneur has brought you considerable wealth. How do you personally see the relationship between biblical and, more specifically, Calvinist teachings and wealth?

23. Is personal wealth also a token of God's grace?

Entrepreneurs & society

24. As a successful entrepreneur do you feel a responsibility to play a visible and active role in society? Or is your first and only responsibility to merely concentrate on your company?

25. What has been the nature of your involvement in civic affairs?

26. Many successful Dutch-American entrepreneurs share Republican political beliefs, traditional family values and conservative moral convictions. Does this also hold for your personal beliefs, values, and convictions?

27. It is well known that you as a highly successful entrepreneur donate substantially to charity. What is the main philosophy behind your involvement and how does this relate to your personal values and beliefs?

That was the last question. Thank you very much!

Duration of interview: _____ minutes